Pat —
This is the book you had posted about wanting to read. I am happy that it has worked out to get it to you. 😊

It's an interesting read, although a little wordy. I appreciate your interest in this & the heart you have for the world, and the love you show to me. Blessings & love —

Amy Dingman

INDIA'S MUSLIM SPRING

INDIA'S MUSLIM SPRING

Why is Nobody Talking about It?

Hasan Suroor

RAINLIGHT
RUPA

Published in Rainlight
by Rupa Publications India Pvt. Ltd 2014
7/16, Ansari Road, Daryaganj
New Delhi 110002

Sales centres:
Allahabad Bengaluru Chennai
Hyderabad Jaipur Kathmandu
Kolkata Mumbai

Copyright © Hasan Suroor 2014

All rights reserved.
No part of this publication may be reproduced, transmitted,
or stored in a retrieval system, in any form or by any means,
electronic, mechanical, photocopying, recording or otherwise,
without the prior permission of the publisher.

ISBN: 978-81-291-3098-3

First impression 2014

10 9 8 7 6 5 4 3 2 1

The moral right of the author has been asserted.

Printed at Replika Press Pvt. Ltd., India

This book is sold subject to the condition that it shall not, by way
of trade or otherwise, be lent, resold, hired out, or otherwise circulated,
without the publisher's prior consent, in any form of binding or cover
other than that in which it is published.

For my parents
Abbu and Ammi
from whom I learned to respect cultural differences

Contents

Prologue ... ix

1 Taken for Granted ... 1
2 Smell the Air ... 19
3 Measuring Change ... 27
4 'Don't Judge Us by Our Beards' ... 32
5 Phoney Fundamentalism ... 37
6 Beyond Mullahs and Marxists ... 47
7 The 'New' Muslim Woman ... 53
8 The Shah Bano Effect ... 59
9 Shahi Imam Who? ... 68
10 A Legacy of Ayodhya ... 77
11 The Rushdie Test ... 87
12 The Muslim Experience ... 91
13 A 'Witch-Hunt' ... 97
14 The Pakistan Connection ... 107
15 Victimhood Syndrome ... 114
16 The Enemy Within ... 118
17 Needed: New Ways of Seeing ... 124
18 The Way Forward ... 131

Part II
In Their Own Words ... 137
Postscript ... 179

Appendix 1	181
Appendix 2	186
Appendix 3	189
Appendix 4	191
Appendix 5	198
Acknowledgements	199

Prologue

Then and Now

When my parents arrived in Delhi from Lucknow in the early 1950s, the Muslim-majority areas of Old Delhi were the natural habitat of Muslims, for the simple reason that these were still early days after the Partition riots and Hindu-Muslim relations were tense, to put it mildly. Muslims were neither welcome nor felt secure in the new suburban neighbourhoods (the so-called 'colonies') populated by Hindu refugees from Pakistan. After failing to find a flat in New Delhi, my parents ended up in one of the many glorified Muslim ghettoes in the walled city.

It was thus that I spent the early years of my life in Ballimaran, a maze of narrow lanes and by-lanes just down the road from 'Ghalib ki Haveli', where the great 19th century Urdu poet Mirza Ghalib had lived. Reading Salman Rushdie's memoirs, *Joseph Anton*, I discovered that Ballimaran had been home to his grandfather Khwaja Muhammad Din Khaliqi Dehalvi, who he describes as a 'successful industrialist and part-time essayist'. He writes that Dehalvi lived in a 'crumbling haveli in the famous old muhalla, or neighbourhood, of Ballimaran, a warren of small winding lanes off Chandni Chowk that had been the home of the great Farsi and Urdu poet, Ghalib'. Who would have thought that one day his grandson would write a book which would be burnt in Muslim ghettoes like

Ballimaran, and his effigies dragged through its 'small winding lanes' amid chants of 'Death to Rushdie'.

Ballimaran was dotted with mosques referred to as 'choti masjid', 'badi masjid', 'phatak wali masjid' after their size and location. They attracted few worshippers except on Fridays or on other special occasions such as Eid—and were valued more as real-estate assets than places of worship.

When I look back, the thing that strikes me the most is that despite a culture that verged on social and cultural fundamentalism (Muslim women, like my mother, who didn't wear burqa faced abuse and had their morals questioned), there was very little religious fervour among the denizens of Ballimaran outside a small circle of 'mullahs'. Near-deserted mosques and idle 'imams' bore testimony to a distinct lack of religiosity among Muslims, especially the young who deliberately avoided mosques around prayer time for fear of being dragged in by their elders.

Another interesting aspect was that although memories of Partition were still raw and Hindu-Muslim relations extremely fraught, there was no talk of asserting a Muslim identity. Women wore burqa ('hijab' is a recent phenomenon) not out of choice—as 'modern' Muslim women do to announce their religious identity—but because they were forced to. And, most got rid of them the moment they thought nobody was watching. Similarly, a beard was not something that men flirted with to flaunt their 'Muslim-ness'. If anything, young Muslims went out of their way *not* to have a beard, to demonstrate their 'modernity'.

Yet, today, when I go to Ballimaran I have to struggle to find a young Muslim who doesn't have a beard. 'Hijab' has replaced the burqa, and Muslim women insist that they wear it of their own volition, often in the face of opposition from their mothers who fought against the veil. At prayer time, mosques are spilling over with young Muslims who have taken time off from work to offer namaz. And this is happening not only in Ballimaran. Long-neglected masjids all over Delhi—and in cities and towns across India—are attracting bigger, newer and younger congregations.

There is a new religiosity in the air, especially among the Muslim youth. Their enthusiasm for Ramadan—a whole long month of fasting—beats me. Young boys and girls voluntarily and cheerfully observe fast day after day for 30 days, even at the height of an Indian summer. My generation, on the other hand, was notorious for avoiding rozas. We drew the line at the obligatory coming-of-age first roza when, for a day, we were treated like royalty.

Even more surprising is the growing clamour for 'hajj'. I have come across 'hajis' as young as twenty-somethings, and by the time they are forty, some have done it more than once. There was a time when it was the last thing people did (if they could afford it, that is) just before they thought they were about to kick the bucket.

Being a Muslim these days means wearing your 'Muslim-ness' on your sleeve. And this extends to the way Muslims greet each other. I grew up in a culture where the more secular 'adaab' was the norm, but these days they insist on 'salaam-alekum' (God is great) and regard it 'un-Islamic' if you don't respond with 'walle-kum-assalam'. My mother never quite got used to 'this naya fashion', as she called it. I still instinctively say 'adaab', and often get dirty looks for it.

Muslims have also become more fussy about what they eat. It was always the case that they ate only 'halal' meat at home, but when dining out—for instance at weddings or parties—they let their guard down. Nobody ever asked where the meat came from; or how the lamb or the chicken was slaughtered. Pork was the only no-go area. But the newly devout Muslim is so paranoid that he/she might make the blunder of eating non-halal meat that they stick to a strict vegetarian diet while travelling or eating out. I know people who would rather starve than eat a vegetarian meal at home, but are suddenly transformed into pure vegetarians when eating out.

But let me pause here for I can hear Muslim-baiters gloat, 'But we told you so—Muslims have gone from bad to worse; they have become more insular, more regressive, and more fundamentalist.'

Well, hold on. They haven't. Religious, yes. More conscious of their identity, certainly. But 'insular, regressive, and fundamentalist'? Emphatically, no. On the contrary, the younger generation of Muslims is more inclusive, more cosmopolitan and more forward-looking than their parents' generation was. Don't judge them by their beards and hijabs. Go and talk to them, which is what I did, and you might be surprised, as I was, to discover how well-adjusted, optimistic and nationalistic today's Indian Muslim youth is. These young men and women (the 18–35 age group) are, no doubt, more religious and deeply conscious of their Muslim identity—a reaction to the post-9/11 Islamophobia—but their worldview is secular. They see themselves as citizens of a secular country and seek no special concessions on account of their minority status, except the courtesy of not to be discriminated against because of their religion.

Admittedly, my research is limited to the educated urban youth, but let's not forget that while India may be living in its villages, ultimately the national mood is shaped by what happens in its cities and towns. It is the young Muslim men and women in the metros who will drive the change if the community is to move forward. And it is already happening. There is a quiet but historic shift taking place in the Muslim mood, driven by a new generation that does not suffer from the sort of hang-ups that previous generations did.

Today's lot too has grievances—mostly to do with anti-Muslim prejudice—but it has a more grown-up approach to dealing with them. Many told me that 'going on and on' about grievances would not help. Muslims must shed their 'siege mentality', stop blaming others for their problems, and take their destiny in their own hands.

'Can we deny that we have neglected education? Can we deny that we lack aspiration? Can we deny that we have not done enough ourselves, as a community, to stand up and address our problems?' asked Jameel Mian, a young Muslim businessman who runs a poultry farm near Meerut.

Sadia Khan, a research scholar at Jamia Millia Islamia, said many Muslims still lived in the past and harped on the 'glories' of the Mughal era. They made no effort to move with the times.

'Look at the Parsi community. Barely a hundred thousand, they have managed to retain their cultural individuality while being part of the national mainstream. They enjoy fame and status out of all proportion to their numbers,' she said.

I discovered a refreshing mood of self-introspection and a willingness to face up to the community's own failings. Voices such as Jameel and Sadia's are the kind of voices I had been dying to hear, but had almost given up on. One reason why much of the outside world doesn't even know that such voices exist is that they are effectively blacked out by the media. For one thing, stories about introspection and community-building make boring news compared to fire-and-brimstone fatwas—and I say this as a weather-beaten journalist who has personal experience of this sort of thing. But there is also a political agenda at work here. Which is, to promote a negative image of Muslims and portray them only as fatwa-spewing, book-burning vandals. Watching Indian television channels, it seems there is a rule of thumb to keep out Muslims who do not fit this image. Major English-language national newspapers do often tend to make an effort to project moderate Muslim voices, but the vast majority of both print and electronic media are interested only in the extreme fringe.

This book is an attempt to provide a corrective to the often deliberately peddled negative perceptions of Muslims, and to highlight the profound change in Muslim thinking. There are a number of excellent academic studies on Indian Muslims but no first-hand, good old-fashioned reporter's account of the new awakening in the community. This volume seeks to offer a view from the ground, or 'ground zero', in the fashionable post-9/11 lingo. We get to hear from a cross-section of young Muslims themselves what it means to be a Muslim in India today, and how they see their future. Arguably, these are not 'typical' Muslim voices and large swathes of the Muslim community continue to answer to the popular stereotype but, at last, I see the first stirrings of a Muslim spring.

But here's a warning: it could still go all belly-up if the new mood in the Muslim community is not matched by a change in the Indian state's institutional mindset, which, as most recently documented by the Sachar Committee, remains mired in anti-Muslim prejudice resulting in an almost apartheid-style denial of equal opportunities to Muslims—and compounded by a policy of harassment by security services in the name of fighting terror. If the Indian state is serious about defeating Muslim fundamentalism, this is surely the wrong way to go about it. It's a moment of truth for all those who have been urging Muslims to take a stand against fundamentalism. Now that they have taken up the challenge, the last thing they need is any provocation that could be seized by the Muslim Right to bounce back. If there ever was a time for an avowedly secular state to put its money where its mouth is, it is now.

1
Taken for Granted

First some dry facts, which, though well-known, are generally glossed over in the often-skewed debate on Indian Muslims. The result is a series of assiduously-promoted myths, the most misleading being that Muslims constitute a monolithic entity on the basis that they belong to the same religion. This, in turn, has spawned the notion of a pan-Islamic Muslim brotherhood based on a common religious identity which supposedly supersedes a Muslim's national identity and the unique cultural characteristics that go with it. The idea that an Indian Muslim will have more in common with a Saudi or a Kuwaiti Muslim than with a fellow non-Muslim Indian is a lot of nonsense. Yet it persists, with Muslims being routinely asked to clarify whether they are 'Indians first' or 'Muslims first'.

All Muslims, it is suggested, think alike, behave alike, and vote alike. In effect, one Muslim is a clone of another Muslim with no distinction between urban Muslims and rural Muslims; educated Muslims and non-educated Muslims; fundamentalist Muslims and moderate Muslims. It is not rare to hear people say: 'Sab mussalman ek se hain' (all Muslims are the same). Then there is the notion of Indian Muslims as 'children' of Mughal invaders, often expressed in crude terms like 'Babar ki aulad', forgetting that India's Muslim links go back long before the Mughals arrived as conquerors.

So, here are the facts. There are an estimated 177 million Muslims in India, comprising more than 14 per cent of its population (official analysis of the 2011 census data on religion is awaited at the time of writing), and representing the world's third largest Muslim community. There are more Muslims in India than in most Muslim countries including Saudi Arabia, the self-styled custodian of Islam. It is a diverse and 'an extremely divided community along the bases of caste, sect and region, like the majority religious community, the Hindus', as Abdul Shaban, Associate Professor at Centre for Development Studies, Tata Institute of Social Sciences, Mumbai, points out in his book, *Lives of Muslims in India: Politics, Exclusion and Violence* (Routledge, 2012).

There are vast cultural differences among Muslims depending upon which part of India they live in. For instance, there is a marked north-south divide, with Muslims in South India having more in common with south Indian Hindus than with their co-religionists in the north. Even within north India, cultural practices among Muslims vary from one region to another. The same is true of Muslims from other regions. Different levels of education and social awareness in different parts of India means that Muslims in south India, West Bengal and Maharashtra are better educated, more moderate and socially liberal than Muslims in north India.

Muslims are also divided internally into two major sects: the Shias and the Sunnis, the latter being in a majority. Despite a common Islamic identity they are so different from each other that even their religious rituals and ways of worship are not the same. Besides, Shias are regarded as socially more liberal with better levels of education and social awareness. These two sects are further divided into sub-sects such as the

Hanafis, the Malikis, the Barelvis and the Deobandis. Within these sub-sects too there are different shades of opinions, as there would be in any group of thinking people. If this is not diversity, we need to redefine the term diversity.

As Shaban says: 'Muslims in India are like any other citizen but only differentiated by a set of belief systems...(yet) the attempt remains to depict Muslims as a monolithic community to enhance the political productivity of the Muslim identity.'

The above snapshot of the cultural and social make-up of India's Muslim community should refute the myth of Muslims as a monolithic group in which all Muslims are reduced to a religious and cultural version of Siamese twins. I deal with this issue at greater length later in the book.

Equally fallacious and misleading is the image of Indian Muslims as 'Babar-ki-aulad'. India's links with Islam go back as early as the 7th century AD, and Muslims first came to India not as invaders but as traders. The first ship carrying Muslim travellers was seen on the Indian coast as early as 630 AD, according to the 19th century British historians Henry Miers Eliot and John Dawson in their book, *The History of India as Told by its Own Historians: The Muhammadan Period*, still regarded as a seminal work on medieval Indian history. The fact that it was trade rather than a campaign to spread Islam in India through conquest is corroborated by other historians such as H.G. Rawlinson (*Ancient and Medieval History of India*) and J.Sturrock (*South Kanara and Madras Districts Manuals*).

But that is ancient history. For the purposes of the current debate on the status of Indian Muslims and Hindu-Muslim relations—the focus of this book—the truly cataclysmic event was the Partition of India in 1947 and the creation of Pakistan following a long politically and emotionally charged campaign by the All-India Muslim League under Mohammed Ali Jinnah for a separate Muslim homeland. The bloody consequences of Partition, with up to a million people on both sides killed in violent clashes and some 12 million displaced in the largest mass migration in human history, are too well-known to bear repetition here. Its legacy means that more than 60 years later, Hindu-Muslim relations remain fraught. Although young Hindus and Muslims are relatively more relaxed about it than previous generations, who directly suffered its consequences, the ghost of Partition continues to hover in the background—and its potential for being politically exploited by the Hindu Right to taunt Muslims remains strong.

Moreover many of the problems of social and economic backwardness of Indian Muslims, can be traced directly to Partition. Pakistan was the creation of a Muslim elite which saw their political and economic interests served better if they had their own independent country rather than in a 'Hindu India'. Among its most staunch supporters were large Muslim landowning families in the Punjab and Sindh, who—according to British historian Crispin Bates—'saw it as an opportunity to prosper within a captive market free from competition'. Thus, the Muslims who migrated to Pakistan represented the cream of undivided India's Muslim society—feudal gentry, civil servants, diplomats, top army brass, businessmen, bankers and other professionals whose skills would be in demand in a new country. The Muslims who were left in India either by choice or circumstances were mostly the 'rump'—petty shopkeepers, self-employed daily wagers like rickshaw pullers, tonga drivers, masons, carpenters, and low-rung government employees like peons, clerks, drivers. They were mostly conservative, lacking social or political awareness, and led miserable insular lives with little or no aspiration. The flight of the Muslim middle class, the engine of upward mobility and progress in any society, to Pakistan, left a big hole at the heart of the Indian Muslim community. The ranks of tall Muslim leaders who could inspire and motivate the community were also hugely depleted. In fact, there was no credible Muslim political leadership left in large parts of India. A few ministers at the centre, which was ruled by the Congress until well into the 1970s, were seen as 'show pieces' whom the rest of the community did not see as their true representatives. They were largely perceived as crumbs thrown to the community in the name of Muslim representation.

It was this vacuum that allowed local mullahs and provincial political operators to take over the reins of a leaderless and demoralised community mired in poverty and illiteracy. They played on its fears and insecurities to emerge as its 'protectors' developing, in the process, a vested interest in keeping it backward. For it is easier to manipulate a weak and vulnerable people. Once they become strong and self-confident, they start asking inconvenient questions of the leadership.

Typically, these self-styled 'leaders' used that most trusted of the opiates of the masses—religion—to keep the community occupied at the expense of what should have been its real priorities: education, jobs and security. No wonder, 66 years after independence they remain at the bottom of the heap as documented by the Sachar Committee, a high-level panel set up by Prime Minister Manmohan Singh under the chairmanship of Justice Rajindar Sachar, retired Chief Justice of the Delhi High Court, to study the 'Social, Economic and Educational Status of the Muslim Community of India', and which gave its report in 2006. There is an irony here: although Indian Muslims are often accused of extra-territorial loyalties to Pakistan it is often overlooked that they have had to pay a heavy price for the creation of Pakistan. Had there been no Partition, the whole composition of the Indian Muslim community would have been very different giving it a political and economic clout that it now lacks. It would have been twice its current size with a strong educated and professional middle class and a leadership of quite a different qualitative order than today's Muslim leadership. The tragedy is that even Pakistan did not quite turn out to be the Muslim paradise it was envisaged to be. Muslims on both sides have had to pay for the original sin of Partition. What form Hindu-Muslim relations might have taken in an undivided India would remain in the realm of contra-factual history, but what is not in doubt is that the story of Indian Muslims would have had a much happier ending without Partition.

Crude Stereotyping

Facts about the history of Indian Islam and the issue of Muslim identity have been manipulated for political purposes to create a narrative that stereotypes Muslims, and then to use those stereotypes to damn—and exploit—them. To be a Muslim in India today means to be perceived as one or more of the following things: an unreconstructed fundamentalist; insular; alienated from the national mainstream; a potential extremist; a closet Pakistani (Muslim-dominated areas are routinely dubbed 'chhota' or 'mini Pakistan'); a Saudi client flush with petro-dollars and on a mission to promote an ultra-conservative version of Islam.

I could go on. This is just a quick checklist of the popular perception of Indian Muslims. And to be honest there are Muslims who answer to one or more of these descriptions and I hold no brief for them. What is, however, deeply troubling is the glib assumption that somehow all or most Muslims are fanatics and that there is no such thing as a sane, moderate Muslim outside of the small liberal left-wing elite which is so way out of sync with the wider community as to be beyond the pale. When I tell people that I also happen to be a Muslim but I don't fit into any of these categories, I am told: 'But you're not a typical Muslim'.

In other words, a 'typical' Muslim is, by definition, backward and fundamentalist and symbolizes the whole community, while a sane Muslim is an exception. This is crude stereotyping and as unfair to Muslims as it would be to Hindus if all of them were to be tarred with the same brush on account of the behaviour of some of their co-religionists. Foreign correspondents often resort to lazy shorthand to describe complicated situations in a way which has the effect of linking an entire community to the actions of a few blacksheep. I remember protesting to a senior BBC journalist for describing the thugs behind the demolition of Babri Masjid on December 6, 1992 as 'Hindu nationalists'. I argued that those fanatics represented neither the wider Hindu community nor any self-respecting nationalist. It was an act committed by a small group of fanatics in the name of Hindu nationalism, but that did not make every Hindu a raving Bajrang Dal supporter.

The mosque, built by the first Mughal emperor, Babur, in 1527 in the eastern Uttar Pradesh town of Ayodhya, was destroyed by a mob of right-wing Hindus with links to the Bhartatiya Janata Party (BJP), the Vishwa Hindu Parishad (VHP) and Bajrang Dal. Claiming that it was built on the exact spot where Lord Ram was born, they deemed the mosque as an 'insult' to the Hindus and said they wished to build a grand Ram Temple in its place. The demolition was carried out despite a commitment to the Supreme Court that the mosque would not be touched. It was the culmination of a long and divisive nationwide 'Ram Mandir' campaign led personally by the then BJP president, Lal Krishan Advani. More than 2,000 people were killed in riots that followed the demolition.

The BBC journalist's response was that he was broadcasting for a foreign audience which required him to simplify things, but, back in London, it sounded as though all Hindus were on the rampage. I bring this up because much of the anti-Muslim prejudice in India is the result of this sort of casual, unintended, stereotyping. It is so commonplace that often people don't even realize what they are doing. For example, telling a liberal Muslim that he is not 'typical' of his community may sound like an innocuous remark to the person making it (even as I write this I know I may be accused of making an unnecessary fuss) but it isn't. It is a loaded comment on the Muslim mindset. For what it says is that a 'typical' Muslim is, per se, illiberal.

Apart from having a depressing effect on the Muslim psyche and making them retreat further into the shell, such perceptions have influenced the way the political establishment and the government have approached the so-called 'Muslim Question'. Instead of treating it as a problem of economic and educational backwardness, and devising policies to address it, there is a tendency to look at it through a distorted cultural prism. Thus, Muslims battling discrimination in jobs and housing, are portrayed as victims of their own regressive cultural attitudes rooted in their religious beliefs. The very term 'Muslim' has come to acquire a negative connotation because of persistent stereotyping. There is anecdotal evidence that a red light starts to flash when employers see a Muslim name on a job application. A few years ago a Mumbai-based academic journal tried a small experiment to assess the scale of discrimination against Muslims. It sent out two sets of identical applications in response to several job advertisements: both sets contained exactly the same CV but the name of the applicant was changed. One was sent in the name of a Muslim candidate and the other carried a Hindu name. The response was telling: most of the applications with Muslim names remained unanswered while identical applications with Hindu names resulted in interview calls.

Similar experiments conducted in Britain to gauge racial discrimination have shown that non-white candidates are routinely ignored in favour of white candidates despite both having identical qualifications. Such discrimination—whether against Muslims in India or non-whites in Britain—has a lot to do with the stereotypical images of these communities ('lazy' blacks, 'charlatan' Pakistanis, 'shifty' Arabs, 'free-booting' east Europeans) invented and propagated by their detractors.

A charge routinely thrown at Muslims is that they don't want to join the 'national mainstream', and that this is what leads to their 'alienation'. 'Not guilty', say Muslims. On the contrary, they point out, the fact is that no serious attempt has been made to draw them into the national mainstream. They see themselves as a casualty of a politics of exclusion whereby they have been actively shut out from state institutions through overt and covert discrimination—a fact comprehensively documented by the Sachar Committee.

In *Lives of Muslims in India: Politics, Exclusion and Violence*, Abdul Shaban argues that 'the sense of alienation from the state among Muslims has been growing as more State institutions are turning communal, and the representation of Muslims in these institutions is dwindling'. He says the Indian state has not been even-handed in its approach to 'marginalized communities'. While it has done a lot to empower non-Muslim marginalized groups, it has neglected the Muslims.

'For instance, a considerable empowerment of Hindu/Buddhist/Sikh dalits has taken place since independence, and their rights have been enshrined and established through the innovation of new laws and formation of new institutions. This is why the dalits see the state as resourceful, while a larger section of Muslims find it repressive, oppressive and discriminatory. To a large extent, Muslims are not only unwelcome in sensitive state services but also find it difficult to get a job in ordinary state-run institutions,' he writes.

The Sachar Committee report, by far the most definitive study of the condition of Indian Muslims, produces statistical data from the government's own agencies, to reveal shocking levels of institutional anti-Muslim bias in almost all areas of public life, and especially in government organizations. Such is the Muslim mistrust of state agencies, according to the report, that they feel uncomfortable even approaching them. Such visible 'markers' of Muslim identity as beard, topi (skullcap) or burqa 'have very often been a target for ridiculing the community as well as looking upon them with suspicion', it points out.

'Muslim men donning a beard and a topi are often picked up for interrogation from public spaces like parks, railway stations and markets. Some women who interacted with the Committee informed how, in corporate offices, Hijab wearing Muslim women were finding it increasingly difficult to find jobs. Muslim women in burqa complain of impolite treatment in the market, in hospitals, in schools, in accessing public facilities such as public transport and so on,' the report says.

Confirming the extent to which Muslim identity has become a barrier to accessing basic needs, it notes: 'Muslim identity affects everyday living in a variety of ways that ranges from being unable to rent/buy a house to accessing good schools for their children. Buying or renting property in localities of one's choice is becoming increasingly difficult for Muslims. Apart from the reluctance of owners to rent/sell property to Muslims, several housing societies in 'non-Muslim' localities 'dissuade' Muslims from locating there.'

There is more in the same vein—paragraphs after depressing paragraphs detailing the daily humiliations that Indian Muslims face.

There is only one way to describe the findings: an unqualified indictment of the Indian state for failing to fulfill its constitutional obligation to protect minority groups from discrimination and to instill in them a sense of security. This is not the first time that the secular credentials of state agencies, particularly the Police, in protecting Muslims have been called into question. The B.N. Srikrishna Commission of Inquiry into the 1992-93 riots in Mumbai, which took place in the wake of the Babri Masjid demolition, revealed that the Police showed deliberate anti-Muslim bias in dealing with the rioters. In its report, the Commission pointedly noted that the police's attitude was, 'one Muslim killed is one Muslim less'. The Commission noted that there was a 'built-in bias of the police force against Muslims'.

'The response of the Police to appeals from desperate victims, particularly Muslims, was cynical and utterly indifferent.

On occasions, the response was that they were unable to leave the appointed post,' it concluded. The Commission went further and held that activists of Shiv Sena, which then ruled Maharashtra in alliance with the BJP, orchestrated the violence against Muslims.

'From January 8, 1993, at least, there is no doubt that the Shiv Sena and Shiv Sainiks took the lead in organising attacks on Muslims and their properties under the guidance of several leaders,' it said. It described Sena chief Bal Thackeray as the 'veteran general commanding his loyal Shiv Sainiks to retaliate by organised attacks against Muslims'.

Jyoti Punwani, a Mumbai-based journalist who covered the proceedings of the Commission, has documented what she describes as the 'consciously partisan' attitude ('pro-Hindu and anti-Muslim') of the Police in a booklet—'Witnesses Speak'— based on the evidence presented before the commission. She has described the proceedings as a 'rare opportunity to discover how the mind of the Police works'.

The state government summarily rejected the Commission's findings calling the report 'anti-Hindu, pro-Muslim and biased'.

Back in the 1960s and 1970s, there were numerous inquiries into the role of the Police and local administration in communal riots in western and central U.P. towns of Meerut, Moradabad, Aligarh and Kanpur. But, like the Srikrishna Commission, their reports were never implemented (though, officially, they were not rejected either). Also collecting dust on the shelves of government ministries are reports of a variety of 'fact-finding' panels, and 'high-power' committees and commissions on the plight of Indian Muslims. In 1980, Indira Gandhi appointed a 'High-Power Panel on Minorities' to examine the condition of minorities, but there was no serious follow-up of its recommendations which were strikingly similar to the Sachar Committee's report.

Steve Wilkinson of Yale University writes that 'each new government (except the BJP) has wanted to establish a new commission or committee to differentiate itself from its predecessor (which is usually condemned as 'having done nothing for the minorities') and appeal to minority voters. All these commissions have found pretty much the same thing: minorities are under-represented in government, in primary, secondary and higher education, and in private employment... They all tell a similar story.' (*New Dimensions of Politics in India: The United Progressive Alliance in Power*, Ed Lawrence Saez and Gurharpal Singh, Routledge).

Of the more recent cases, the jury is still out on the extent of the BJP administration's alleged involvement in the 2002 violence in Gujarat, in which hundreds of Muslims were killed. According to a Human Rights Watch report, state officials were directly involved—first in engineering violence and then in a massive cover-up. Several countries snapped ties with the Gujarat Government. Its chief minister Narendra Modi is still banned from visiting America. The Congress-ruled central government of Narasimha Rao was heavily criticized for not doing anything to stop the demolition of Babri Masjid. Mr. Rao and his ministers remained passive spectators as the mosque was demolished in the full glare of television cameras. Mr. Rao was to famously claim later that not taking a decision was also a decision. He said he decided not to act because he believed it could create a serious law and order situation. Muslims regard it as the lowest moment in the history of secular India—and the Congress is still struggling to regain their trust.

Some may find the title of the book puzzling and ask:

What Muslim spring? When did it arrive? And why has there been no mention in the media?

Well, that's exactly the point of this book. Why is nobody talking about the biggest shake-up of the Muslim mind since independence?

There wouldn't be a need for such a book if the media had bothered to look beyond its nose. Instead of getting its news from self-styled Muslim 'leaders'—permanent fixtures on Indian television channels—had the media done a bit of legwork it would have discovered a young generation of educated, articulate and forward-looking Muslims determined to make a clean break with the past, and chart a new course for the community.

American journalist Anne Applebaum has written that in the days before the collapse of communism in Eastern Europe, in the late 1980s and early 1990s, when people were asked what they were striving for, their answer usually was: 'We want to be normal'. The same can be said about Indian Muslims today: they want to be 'normal'. For the east Europeans, of course, to be 'normal' meant to be like their west European peers in terms of individual freedoms, democracy etc.

For India's Muslims 'normal' means to be like other Indian citizens focusing on 'normal' priorities like education, jobs, housing, and security. They have had enough of mandir-masjid disputes and moaning about grievances. And they desperately want to be rid of self-serving 'leaders' and power-brokers in long beards, who they blame for many of the community's ills.

There is a seismic shift taking place in Muslim thinking which, I argue, needs to be taken note of and supported if India really wants a confident, forward-looking and well-adjusted Muslim community in tune with the rest of the society. In other words, a 'normal' community. It is the emerging moderate Muslim voices, not the old guard tainted by association with fundamentalism, which should be projected as the modern face of Indian Muslims. Their genuine concerns around discrimination and security issues must be highlighted and addressed.

It is not easy to sell reforms and change to a community which, thanks to years of indoctrination by a status quo-ist leadership, has given up on the future. The young Muslims campaigning for reform need to have something to show to their pessimistic fellow-Muslims, that moderation works. I have heard Muslims complain that no matter how much they change they would continue to be stereotyped, portrayed as fundamentalists, and discriminated against. They can be disabused of such conspiracy theories if the media and political parties start talking about the changes. This will have an impact on the public view of the Muslim community whose image today is unremittingly negative—a people firmly stuck in the past and unwilling to move forward. Once the battle of perception is won, it will inevitably transform the society's attitude towards Muslims, thereby improving their chances of being treated as 'normal' citizens who can be trusted with jobs, and who you won't mind having as a tenant. For, how a society treats its citizens depends a great deal on how it perceives them. Negative perceptions shape negative responses.

Muslims will have to be assured that change is worth it. The government must do its bit by sending out a message that it is concerned about their problems and is listening to them. Implementing at least some of the major recommendations of the Sachar Committee, such as steps to boost recruitment of Muslims in government jobs, eliminating discrimination, and providing them greater access to educational and economic opportunities will be a good start.

Prejudice and Ignorance

My experience of reporting and commenting on Hindu-Muslim relations has convinced me of one thing: neither side likes to be told the truth. The same set of people—whether Muslim or Hindu—who would come to you and say, 'Well done', when you criticize the other side are quick to turn on you for making even the most feeble criticism of their own community. I have had my share of brickbats—accused by Muslims of 'selling out', and by Hindus of being 'anti-national' and 'showing my Muslim colours', whatever that might mean. I have often been in situations (recounted in the book) which would have been funny had they not revealed the deep-seated sectarian divide that still exists between the two communities, more than six decades after Partition. Although a new post-Partition generation is making a brave and determined effort to draw a line under the past, Hindu-Muslim understanding of each other is still coloured by prejudice rooted partly in a sectarian reading of history, and partly in ignorance.

Given a shared history, going back several centuries, the level of mutual ignorance about each other's culture—festivals and customs—is simply staggering, and has led to mistrust and suspicion. Politicians have further muddied the waters. Barring the Left, political parties of all hues have shamelessly exploited Hindu-Muslim differences to build their respective vote banks. While the Congress has cynically played on Muslim fears and insecurities to garner their votes by posing as their protector, the right-wing Hindu parties such as the Bharatiya Janata Party and

Shiv Sena have sought to cultivate the Hindu vote by raising the bogey of Muslim 'appeasement', and claiming that Hindus are being discriminated in their 'own' country.

While it is all too easy to blame the politicians, ultimately it is for the two communities themselves to put the past behind them and embark on a more constructive course of engagement with each other, thus preventing politicians from exploiting their differences. Both communities need to reach out to each other by shedding their prejudices and showing greater understanding of each other's social and cultural practices. Muslims need to get out of their 'siege mentality' and stop seeing conspiracies everywhere. They also need to be more pragmatic while pressing their demands. They must face up to the fact that they are in a minority and, like minorities anywhere in the world, they will face pressures. The way to deal with them is not through confrontation or by going into a sulk, but through accommodation and compromise. After all, it is they who stand to lose more in any confrontation, as we have seen again and again, than the majority community. The Hindus, as the larger and stronger group—numerically, politically and economically—need to learn to be more magnanimous towards their fellow minority citizens. An educationally and economically strong minority is good for the whole country. It is in nobody's interest to have more than 170 million citizens stuck in illiteracy, poverty and a cultural time-warp. For, ultimately, they are a drain on the entire system and drag everyone down with them. The social and economic backwardness of Muslims has been a subject of endless debate since independence but they still lag behind on every measure of social, economic and cultural progress, as revealed by the Sachar Committee. Seven years after it gave its report, it is still being debated.

The issue of Muslim fundamentalism—their attitude towards women, intolerance of free speech and an obsession with religious identity—is also linked to the community's backwardness, which has allowed the mullahs to take over its leadership. Indeed Indian Muslims' fundamentalism is driven less by religious fervor than by a retrograde mindset arising from a lack of education and economic development. Unlike in Pakistan and Bangladesh, Muslims in India have never seriously campaigned for introduction of sharia or anti-blasphemy laws. They have only been opposed to the imposition of a uniform civil code arguing that Muslims who wish to be governed by the Muslim Personal Law to settle family matters such as marriage, divorce and property rights, should be allowed to do so. But even on this issue there is a wide split in the community, with a significant section of progressive Muslims, especially women, in favour of a common secular law for all.

In the following pages, I attempt to debunk some of the myths about Muslim fundamentalism, analyse issues that have shaped Muslim thinking since independence, and look at the way forward in the light of some very profound changes that are taking place in the community. I show how these changes have been willfully ignored by the media and the political class. My contention is that a distorted reading of the problems of Indian Muslims has contributed to a situation where so many decades after independence the 'Muslim Question' is still staring us in the face—like an ugly running sore.

2
Smell the Air

Let me confess that this is not the book I set out to write. The book I had in mind was about the unchanging face of Muslim fundamentalism in India. But barely a few weeks into research, I discovered that I was completely on the wrong track. The big story staring me in the face was quite the opposite—that is, far from flourishing, Muslim fundamentalism was actually dying a slow death. As I travelled across the country and spoke to people, I found that over the past decade (the period when I had been away from India) there had been a profound change in the Muslim mindset. Today's Indian Muslim, I discovered, was altogether a different species—educated, aware, wiser, less sectarian and more pragmatic—than the one I had known for much of my life.

Away from the sensational headlines about Islamic extremism, a quiet revolution is taking place. The Muslim discourse has moved on from an obsessive focus on sectarian demands (does anyone remember the last big debate on Muslim Personal Law, for example?) to the more secular bread-and-butter issues. Where once the dinner table talk in Muslim households was unremittingly negative and pessimistic (it was all about how Muslims were being 'crushed' and trampled upon, and had no future in India), today it is about change and looking forward. There is a new optimism abroad that is hard to miss. What is significant is that the change is being urged upon not by the usual suspects—the agnostic left-wing Muslim intellectuals answering the description of Jean Paul Sartre's 'inauthentic' Muslim—but by 'gold-plated' practising Muslims, deeply conscious of their Muslim identity and unapologetic about flaunting it.

There is a new generation of Muslims who want to rid the community of its insular and sectarian approach by concentrating on things that affect their everyday lives: education, jobs, housing, security. They despair of mullahs and self-styled Muslim 'leaders'. And they speak a language that is modern and forward-looking. Their interpretation of Islam stresses inclusion and tolerance. They abhor the use of violence in the name of Islam. They may not be wildly enthusiastic about the western notion of free speech and, without exception, believe that *The Satanic Verses* is an offensive book. Some even tend to share the conspiracy theories about Salman Rushdie's alleged motives, but they condemn the campaign of intimidation and harassment to which he has been subjected in the name of 'defending' Islam and the Prophet. They are embarrassed by such antics which, they say, bring shame to the community and, indeed, Islam itself. There is a feeling of having been let down by previous generations—their parents, grandparents—who they believe were too timid to challenge the fundamentalists. 'We want to draw a line under all that and move on,' is a common refrain.

Notably, it is the young women, often in 'hijab', who are driving the change. Contrary to the stereotyped image of the 'Muslim woman', they are educated, articulate, conscious of their rights and have aspirations that are no different from those of any other modern Indian woman. I found them more progressive in many respects than their male peers. And their struggle is greater as they are engaged, simultaneously, on two fronts—challenging the male Muslim orthodoxy and, at the same time, fighting for a wider change in the community that they hope would alter the prevailing negative perceptions of Muslims.

Paradoxically, at one level this is also perhaps the most religious post-independence generation of Indian Muslims—'pucca namazis' many of whom have already performed 'hajj', some more than once. More Muslim youth wear beards today than ever before, and young Muslim women proudly show off their 'hijabs'. There is a shameless obsession with symbols of Muslim identity that can be quite irritating. Yet, it is also the most open-minded and self-confident generation; and—most importantly—optimistic about its future in India. India is their home and this is where they see their future.

'It is the best place in the world,' is a phrase that I heard over again and again. For all the talk of Muslim 'alienation', today's young Muslims are remarkably well-integrated and see themselves as an integral part of the so-called 'national mainstream' rather than as a separate interest group that they are portrayed as—a perception for which previous generations of Muslims bear some responsibility. Today's young see no contradiction in being proud practicing Muslims and, at the same time, proud secular Indians. They find it insulting to be asked whether they regard themselves as Muslims first or Indians first. To them the question smacks of the questioner's own prejudices. On the Muslim street, it is dismissed as a 'bogus' debate contrived to force Muslims to choose between their religion and their country—a choice that Hindus are not asked to make.

'It is a false choice that we are asked to make. Call me an

Indian Muslim or a Muslim Indian, it makes no difference. When I'm abroad and people ask me my nationality I simply say I'm an Indian, but when they ask me my religion I say I'm Muslim. It's as simple as that. There is no question of one taking priority over the other,' said Ishrat Jahan, a hotel executive.

In the fashionable lingo of the day, Indian Muslims are having their own 'spring'. It may not have the shape of an organised movement, and we may not see people going around waving banners or picketing 'mullahs', but it is genuine, widespread, and it looks like it is here to stay. The media has largely ignored the change that is sweeping India's Muslim community, and continues to play up the extreme voices because they make 'news'. Yet, five or ten years from now, it might realise that it missed the biggest story of its time unfolding right under its nose.

After the Nightmare

Living through the worst phase of Indian Muslim fundamentalism from the 1970s through to the 1990s, I never thought I would live to write its obituary. The depressing prospect of having to live the rest of my life in a climate of competitive Muslim-Hindu fundamentalism, feeding on each other in a toxic double act, was one reason why at an age when many migrants contemplate returning 'home' I decided to take a break from India and moved to Britain. I simply couldn't take it anymore.

At one extreme, there was the creeping 'Hindutva-isation' of India with a resurgent Hindu Right flexing its muscles, and at the other, a wave of Muslim fundamentalism dragging the whole community deeper and deeper into a long dark tunnel of isolation, at the end of which there appeared to be no light. Their actions reinforced the image of Muslims as a backward, intolerant and insular community that refuses to join the 'national mainstream'. With such friends, Muslims didn't need external enemies. It did their work for them. The Babri Masjid fiasco was as much the doing of chest-thumping Muslim 'leadership' as it was a calculated act by the right-wing Hindu middle class, to humiliate Muslims.

Arbitrary 'fatwas' based on the most regressive of interpretations of Islam were commonplace. I heard of more fatwas in the 1990s than I had in the previous half century. Those who didn't agree with the fundamentalist view were denounced, portrayed as closet 'RSS stooge', and hounded.

That was then. A decade later, there is a sea change, thanks to the coming of age of a new generation of Muslims—less excitable and wiser—having learnt from the follies of their predecessors. And certainly more realistic about their place in a Hindu-majority India. All you need to do is to get out a bit more, talk to people, listen to the voices around you, and you'll discover how refreshing the air smells today than it did all those years ago.

The perpetually angry, raving and ranting Muslim fundamentalists who saw anti-Muslim conspiracies everywhere, thrived on whipping up religious hysteria, revelled in Hindu 'provocations', and propagated the most dangerous ideas about Muslim 'identity' have had their day. They are gasping for breath, managing occasionally to stage stunts such as the anti-Salman Rushdie drama at the 2012 Jaipur Literature Festival. The fact—and this went unnoticed amid a hysterical media reaction—that they had few cheerleaders, except for a gaggle of Deoband boys dragged into it by their teachers, showed how little support the agitation had in the wider community.

Rushdie himself described it as a Congress-inspired show aimed at exploiting Muslim sentiments on the eve of state elections in Uttar Pradesh. In the event, the Congress share of Muslim votes actually fell, he noted and complimented the Muslims for not falling into its trap.

Contrast this with the frenzy that followed the publication of *The Satanic Verses* in 1988 (the frenzy continued even after it was banned by the Indian Government) and you will get some idea of how much the community has changed since then, and how isolated the fundamentalists have become. What happened in Jaipur was the last of the hurrahs of a diminishing tribe struggling to make its presence felt. Surely, there will be more such shows of bravado from time to time but it is the bark of a dog that has lost its bite. What we are witnessing is a slow death of Muslim fundamentalism. The community can't wait to pull the plug on it, and to give it a decent burial.

It might sound paradoxical but the only people who will not want Muslim fundamentalism to die are the Hindu fundamentalists. It is their meat and drink—and keeps them supplied with oxygen. Despite a sprinkling of some bright former communists who, opportunistically, embraced the Bharatiya Janata Party (BJP) at the height of the Hindutva wave, the Hindu Right is so pathetically bereft of a coherent ideology or intellectual underpinning that it desperately needs the bogey of minority fundamentalism to justify its existence. Take that away and it would be flailing. There's a very real danger that it would try its utmost to reignite the Muslim Right.

Muslims should beware of this and avoid falling into any trap designed to stoke the dying embers of fundamentalism.

They must learn from their past mistakes when they allowed the 'mullocracy' and its proxies to entrench themselves by raising the bogey of 'Islam in danger' on the back of RSS-inspired Muslim-baiting. Fear-mongers were able to convince a mostly uneducated and insecure community that they alone could 'protect' it from a Hindu assault on its religion and identity. Liberal Muslims, too posh to dirty their hands, watched as conservatives, patronized by a Congress Party desperate to secure minority votes, seized the Muslim agenda.

I don't wish to reopen old wounds because this book is about looking ahead rather than raking up the past, but it is important to put the rise of Muslim fundamentalism in independent India in perspective. Muslim fundamentalism did not grow in a vacuum. Its seeds lay in the way Muslims were treated. There was a systematic attempt to intimidate them and undermine Muslim culture. Those who remember the frequency with which anti-Muslim riots happened through the 1960s and right up to the 1970s, and the way Urdu language was killed (read the Sachar Committee report),would understand what I'm talking about.

I am not discounting the inherent insularity and backwardness of the rump of the Muslim community left behind in India after Partition, but what it needed was a helping hand to steer it into the much talked about 'mainstream'. Instead, Muslims were pushed into a shell as the Hindu Right and the Congress secularists, acting separately but to the same end, fuelled their fears and insecurity. Both had their own vested interests in keeping Muslims in a perpetual state of anxiety and uncertainty. The right-wing Hindu agenda was to frighten them—through a relentless campaign of intimidation—into believing that they were at the 'mercy' of the majority community. A weak and insecure Muslim community also suited the Congress because it could then exploit their anxieties to garner votes in return for a promise to 'protect' them. It was an extortion racket. Plain and simple. And to this end, the Congress created and propped up Muslim leaders—local bullies acting in concert with mullahs—who were little more than glorified pimps. Their job was not to lead the community but to pimp for the Congress: in return for political patronage they delivered Muslims to the Congress.

It is obvious why an aware and economically viable Muslim community does not suit either the Hindu Right or the Congress. The new Muslim awakening is their worst nightmare come true. Suddenly, they face the prospect of losing a constituency that in different ways kept them in business for so long. The warning signals are already up. As fundamentalist cheerleaders for the Congress lose their grip over Muslims, the community has become politically more independent and, as successive elections in recent years have shown, it is no longer willing to be treated as a captive vote bank by any political party. Freed from pressures of self-styled leaders, Muslims have acquired the much-needed political nous to figure out where their interests lie. They do not want to be sucked into a political protection racket again.

When I talk about the decline of Muslim fundamentalism in India I don't claim that the community has been rid of every last fanatic. In fact there are still too many fanatics and mad mullahs around but they are rapidly losing their influence, and, for the first time in post-independent India, the balance of power is rapidly shifting from fundamentalists to the moderates. It is a tectonic shift which, if sustained, could transform the face—and indeed the fortunes—of India's Muslim community for good.

3
Measuring Change

There is no scientific test to measure cultural changes in a community as they happen slowly over a period of time and away from the public gaze. Statistics can tell you whether there has been improvement or decline in a group's socio-economic status, but shed little light on the more abstract and subterranean cultural changes. Good old-fashioned journalism—i.e. talking to as wide a cross-section of people as possible and asking them the right questions—remains the best way to get a drift of the public mood.

My upbeat conclusions about the current Muslim mood are based on an examination of four crucial factors: (1) the Muslim attitude to free speech and dissent; (2) the community's perception of its priorities;(3) its treatment of women; and (4) whether it is willing to take responsibility for its own future.

Indian Muslims have been notoriously vulnerable in these areas: a shamefully high degree of intolerance; grossly misplaced priorities; a contempt for the rights of women verging on misogyny; and a tendency to blame everyone else but themselves for their problems, allowing them to wallow in a sense of victimhood—a tendency that has prevented them from attempting any self-introspection.

It's striking how much the attitudes have changed over the past decade on all these issues. On free speech, no doubt,

Salman Rushdie remains a dirty word for most Muslims, and a perceived attack on Islam, especially the Prophet and the Quran, can still be used to whip up religious passions. A vast majority of Muslims remain extremely sensitive to any criticism of Islam, but except among the usual politically-inspired suspects, there is no more appetite for violence. Nobody wants a book or a film banned, or someone killed for 'insulting' Islam. It is significant that Indian Muslims steered clear of the madness that seized much of the Muslim world, including Pakistan, in September 2012 in the form of murderous protests against the American anti-Islam film *Innocence of Muslims*.

Protests like the anti-Rushdie farce at the 2012 Jaipur festival have little support in the wider Muslim community, which is moving towards a more grown-up approach to perceived 'attacks' on Islam or 'anti-Islamic rant'. 'Peaceful protest yes; but violence no', is the new sensible line.

Tactics apart, there is now a greater awareness of the importance of free speech and creative expression, particularly among the younger generation which is driving the change.

'You can't defend (MF) Hussain's right to paint Hindu gods and goddesses in the nude but cry foul when someone takes liberties with your religious sensitivities. If it is right to vandalize a newspaper office and threaten to kill a cartoonist for 'insulting' the Prophet, then the right-wing Hindu goons who vandalize Hussain's paintings are also right. You can't have double standards on free speech. Either there's such a thing as right to creative expression or there isn't,' said a young struggling Muslim theatre actor.

You might argue that as a creative artiste himself, he would say that, wouldn't he? But it is a view that resonates with a growing number of Muslims, even if some express it crudely—

like a Meerut car dealer who, referring to critics of Islam, said: 'Let the barking dogs bark. Ignore them and they will go away.'

I have dealt with this issue in greater detail in a separate chapter, *The Rushdie Test*.

Equally encouraging is the new Muslim thinking on their priorities, once dictated by fuzzy notions of cultural and religious identity. Albeit belatedly, Muslims have not only become more pragmatic in choosing their priorities, but are willing to make compromises with the 'enemy' if it is in the best interest of the community. This is best illustrated by its attitude towards parties such as the BJP, which it once regarded as untouchable. Today, Muslims are more likely to hold their nose and vote for the BJP if they believe it is in their interest to do so. The growing clamour in the community that it should make peace with Narendra Modi, BJP's divisive Chief Minister of Gujarat, despite his role in the 2002 anti-Muslim violence, illustrates the new mood of pragmatism in the community. They know that if they want to live and prosper in Gujarat they will need to have Modi on their side.

In the 2013 municipal elections in Gujarat, Muslims voted with their feet for the BJP in several areas, with the party pulling off a coup by winning all 27 seats in the Muslim-majority town of Salaya in Dwarka district. In Salaya, Muslims, who form 90 per cent of the population, have benefited from its development under Modi.

Salem Mohammad Baghaad, a traditional Congress activist, who switched sides to contest on a BJP ticket, admitted that it was not an easy choice to make but he took the plunge because it was the only sensible thing to do.

'Honestly, joining the BJP was a tough decision for me. But I was confident about myself, about my decision. I knew if I joined hands with Mr Modi, it will mean more benefits for the town and more development... It was like Narendra Modi opened the government coffers for us. Whatever money we wanted for development came flowing in. And it hasn't stopped,' he said.

What happened in Salaya reflects the increasing recognition among Muslims of the importance of focusing on things that really matter—education, jobs and security. There is an acknowledgement that in the past they allowed emotions to have the better of their sense of priorities.

Young Muslims can barely conceal their anger as they look back at more than half a century of wasted years and determined not to repeat the mistakes of their parents and grandparents. There is a generational shift away from a culture of victimhood and distorted priorities towards introspection, self-reliance and tackling bread-and-butter issues.

By far the most significant development is the rise of a generation of independent, articulate Muslim women who are not afraid to speak their mind and defy the popular caricature of a 'typical' Muslim woman—invariably uneducated or a school dropout; lacking aspiration; happily submissive; and a passive participant in her own oppression.

Statistics on Muslim women's education remain depressing but anecdotal evidence suggests vast improvement. There are few urban middle class homes where there are no school/college/university going women. More significantly, there's an aspirational shift. Young Muslim women are seriously aspiring (instead of simply dreaming as their mothers and grandmothers did) to careers that, until recently, were regarded off-limits for women in conservative families. They are a determined lot, prepared to stand up for their right to be educated and to pursue careers of their choice. There's a new self-confidence among young Muslim women, not seen before outside the circle of a tiny liberal elite.

The Muslim mindset, generally, has changed. Once, talking to Muslims was a depressing experience as all they ever did was moan and groan while wallowing in self-pity. Anyone who disagreed was branded an 'enemy stooge'. A prominent Muslim MP, who gained notoriety for promoting fundamentalist causes, threatened to throw me out of his office because I had the temerity to question his tactics. Such elements still exist but they are no longer mainstream. Yet the media—especially television—and political parties continue to flog them.

For the past 60 years Muslims have faced criticism (and rightly so) for refusing to change. Now that they are trying to do so, we owe it to them to acknowledge it and encourage them. The emerging moderate voices deserve to be applauded and given more space in the media, which for too long has been monopolized by the usual discredited suspects masquerading as Muslim representatives.

The debate on the 'Muslim Question', which is currently focused too narrowly on the community's failings must be opened up to reflect the changes taking place in the community. Political parties and opinion-makers are on test: how they respond to these changes will show whether they are genuinely concerned about the future of Indian Muslims.

4
'Don't Judge Us by Our Beards'

My first appointment for this book was with a young Muslim graphic designer from Delhi. While I waited for him at a coffee shop at the appointed time, he sent me a text message saying he would be delayed slightly because of 'maghrib ki namaaz' (evening prayers) but should be with me soon, 'inshallah'. My heart sank. I had visions of someone in a flowing beard and skull cap, and spouting religious pieties. But when Aqeel Ahmed arrived, slightly breathless and fiddling with a Blackberry, he was nothing like I had imagined: he wore a tweed jacket over an open neck designer shirt and faded blue denim jeans. He did have a beard but it was more Lenin than Imam Bukhari: the sort of person you're more likely to encounter in an up-market bar on an evening than in a mosque.

As we settled down—I with a cup of tea while he ordered cappuccino with 'lots of sugar', and a Danish pastry—Aqeel told me that he was the only 'namaazi' in his family.

'You can call me the odd mullah out in my family,' he joked. Neither of his parents (his father, a retired civil engineer from Madhya Pradesh, and his mother a housewife) was religious and the only sibling—a brother, slightly older than him, was a 'communist'. But he insisted that he had 'no issues' with those who didn't share his enthusiasm about religion, and said he was against attempts to impose religion on others.

'In the end it is between you and your creator, and nobody has any business telling others what or what not to do,' he said.

His own fiancée was 'quite casual' about religion. 'She has no interest in religion but that's her business. I still love her and we will marry in the summer, inshallah.'

But did he view non-practicing Muslims as 'lesser' Muslims? 'I have never thought of it in terms of 'fuller' or 'lesser' Muslims. In any case, it is not for me to judge others.'

How important was his religious identity to him?

'I'm proud of it and quite happy, in your words, to 'flaunt' it. I want to tell the world: look at me I have a beard and I'm a practicing Muslim but I am also educated, a successful professional, and as liberal as anyone else. It is my way of disabusing my non-Muslim friends of the idea that any Muslim in a beard is a fundamentalist. People of other faiths proudly wear religious symbols in public—and quite rightly so. So why should I feel embarrassed or apologetic?'

I asked Aqeel whether he agreed that Muslim women were oppressed and Muslims had become increasingly intolerant of free speech.

'Of course,' he said without hesitation,'and I don't blame the clergy and fundamentalists alone for it. I also have issues with liberal Muslims. They only talk and criticise but don't do anything. Let them roll up their sleeves, dirty their hands…all they do is lecture from the sidelines.'

Finally, I asked him how he would describe himself, and what was it like being a young Muslim in India?

'I would describe myself as a proud Indian Muslim—a modern citizen of a secular and liberal country. This is the only country I know, and I won't go anywhere for love or money. Yes there are problems, and Muslims face prejudice, but I am optimistic that we'll overcome all that, inshallah.'

Would he call himself a 'liberal' Muslim?

'I think it is very patronising to apply such labels. And why is that only Muslims are categorised as liberals and fundamentalists? But since you ask, yes, I would like to believe that I am a liberal even if others may not think so because of my beard and the fact that I go to a masjid five times a day,' he said, and then, after a pause, shot back with some irritation: 'You've been interrogating me for now close to three hours, what do you think? Do I sound like a fundamentalist to you? Don't judge us by our beards, please.'

After the meeting, as he rose to go, Aqeel suggested that I return to India.

'India is the safest and best place for Muslims to live. Do come back,' he said almost beseeching me.

I had to assure him that I had moved abroad for professional reasons and not because I didn't feel safe in India. But, interestingly, it was a sentiment ('India is the best and safest place for Muslims') that I was to hear again and again from young Indian Muslims.

Meanwhile my first, somewhat cynical reaction, as I reviewed my notes of the interview, was that his answers seemed too pat and politically correct. Had he been bluffing me? Feeding me well-rehearsed lines in order to present himself as a 'liberal' and 'modern' young Muslim? So, I ran a background check on him and was happy to discover that Aqeel was for real. In fact, it seemed that he had been rather modest in his claims. I learned that as a university student he was known as a 'Young Turk' for his liberal views, and was once thrown out of a local mosque after he questioned the validity of a fatwa an Imam had issued. He also ran a successful campaign against attempts by conservative student groups to impose a 'dress code' on Muslim students.

So how did he come to have a beard and stuff?

To find out, I met Aqeel's father, Jameel, who introduced himself as the 'original Aqeel', jokingly alluding to his son's strong resemblance to him. He said he himself had been a 'flag-waving agnostic' all his life, and still was. Nor had Aqeel shown any interest in religion until a few years ago. I was amused how Aqeel's father kept saying that his son had been a *'normal* child' till he started showing signs of religiosity.

The reason he gave for Aqeel's 'conversion', as he put it, was one I was to hear repeatedly from others. It was, he said, an 'emotional reaction' to the post-9/11 Islamophobia. He admitted that initially he was very concerned when his son grew a beard, and started talking about Islam and Muslim identity.

'To be honest, we feared that he had been radicalised but, touch wood, it turned out to be nothing of the sort. I am often irritated by his religious habits but now I am very proud of him. He is not only *not* a mullah but anti-mullah. And you will find a lot of young Indian Muslims like him who take religion seriously and, in my view, have a slightly misplaced sense of their identity but are open and broadminded—in some cases more broadminded than the previous generation,' he said.

And, indeed, I did meet a lot of such Muslim youth. Not only in big metros, but in small towns and institutions regarded as hotbeds of Muslim reaction and fundamentalism. I met young Muslims who defended free speech and opposed the ban on Salman Rushdie's *The Satanic Verses*; I met young Muslim women at Aligarh Muslim University (see chapter later) who publicly challenged their conservative male colleagues over their understanding of Islam and Islamic identity; and I met Muslim youth who said events like the demolition of Babri Masjid had been a 'blessing in disguise' for Muslims, in that they had made them 'sit up' and ask hard questions about the real issues facing their community. Almost everyone I met said that despite difficulties they were optimistic about their future in India.

Is this then the 'new' face of the younger generation of Indian Muslims?

Deeply and unapologetically religious and conscious of their identity, but at the same time refreshingly liberal and articulate: a face that defies the popular Muslim stereotype who is either a fundamentalist mullah, with not a liberal or modern bone in his body, or an ultra-secularist liberal who has no time for religion.

5
Phoney Fundamentalism

There is a great deal of confusion about the nature of Indian Muslim fundamentalism. And this confusion is often fuelled deliberately by fundamentalists in an attempt to glorify a phenomenon that is essentially a combination of opportunism, ignorance and reaction as something rooted in Islamic tradition. They pretend to be inspired by some higher religious principles to 'save' Islam from its Hindu 'enemies'. This plays into the hands of their Hindu opponents who seize on it to grease their campaign to demonise Islam. Thus, individual acts of Muslim intolerance and backwardness come to be blamed on Islam.

The fact is that post-independence, Muslim fundamentalism has no theological or intellectual underpinning. Once the two-nation theory, which defined Muslims as a separate 'nation' to justify the demand for a separate Muslim homeland, was taken care of with the creation of Pakistan, the Muslims left behind in India failed to develop an alternative analytical framework to respond to the challenges of 'adaptation and negotiation' (Mushirul Hasan, *Islam in a Globalized World: Negotiating Faultlines*) that they faced in independent India. There was no debate on the way forward, and no attempt to develop a coherent strategy of constructive engagement with the majority community. Progressive Muslims, who should have taken the lead in mobilizing the community around a platform of social justice and freedom, were so wrapped up in their own notions of secularism and so disdainful of anything that smacked of religion, that they happily abandoned it.

It was into this vacuum that the mullahs and their political patrons stepped in with a separatist agenda that saw Muslims withdraw into their shell in the name of protecting their religious and cultural identity. A crude version of identity politics focused on issues like preserving sharia laws, and verging on what one historian has described as 'withdrawal and self-exclusion', took over. And, slowly, the whole edifice of Indian Muslim fundamentalism came to rest on what Salman Rushdie has called the 'reactionary emotional power of grievances'.

What has also happened is that any Muslim who has a grievance, or is vocal about Muslim identity, is promptly dubbed a fundamentalist. I am personally guilty of doing this to my Muslim friends who, for example, oppose forcible imposition of a uniform civil code or get excited about sectarian issues. This has led to an exaggerated view of Muslim fundamentalism, attributing to it a scale and influence it doesn't have.

Here a distinction must be made between the kind of Muslim fundamentalism that underpinned the idea of Pakistan and led to the Partition, and the fundamentalism of those Muslims who, for a variety of reasons (not all to do with nationalism, as I have argued elsewhere), chose to stay back in India. In fact there are sharp differences even over the nature of demand for a separate Muslim homeland, and so many years later a debate is still raging over whether Pakistan was a religious or a political project. The confused nature of the Pakistan project explains why that country still suffers from a debilitating crisis of identity—unable to decide whether it is a modern secular state or a Muslim theocracy that must define itself against a 'Hindu' India.

Its chief architect, Mohammed Ali Jinnah, had no religious pretensions, and it is well-known that he never intended Pakistan to be an Islamic theocratic state. That Jinnah's call for a Muslim nation was simply a political stunt, a means to achieve his political ambitions dressed up in religious terms, is acknowledged even by Hindu nationalists—at least by the less blinkered among them.

In his biography of Jinnah *(Jinnah-India-Partition Independence,* Rupa, 2009), BJP leader Jaswant Singh writes that religion was an 'entirely incidental' element in Jinnah's Pakistan campaign.

'The Muslim community for Jinnah became an electoral body; his call for a Muslim nation his political platform. The battles he fought were entirely political—between the Muslim League and the Congress; Pakistan was his political demand over which he and the Muslim League could rule. Religion in all this was entirely incidental,' he argues.

The school which subscribes to the view that the creation of Pakistan was inspired by Islamic fundamentals is in a minority. Farzana Shaikh, the UK-based Pakistan scholar, is among the few who hold this view. In her controversial book, *Community and Consensus in Islam: Muslim Representation in Colonial India, 1860-1947*(first published by Cambridge University Press in 1989, and recently reprinted in India by imprintOne) she argues that it was the influence of ideas rooted in Islamic tradition that led to the Partition. She questions the popular view that Indian Muslim politics can be explained by reference to pragmatic interests alone. Others, most notably the British Islam scholar Francis Robinson, have highlighted the tension between what Muslims believe should be the 'ideal Muslim life' as laid down in Islam, and the life they actually lead. It is their quest for the 'ideal Muslim life' in a non-Muslim state that accounts for Muslim fundamentalism, according to this argument.

A host of influential Indian and western historians have debunked this thesis, and it remains a minority view. This is not to say that Muslim fundamentalism is completely devoid of religious orthodoxies. No doubt there is a stream of fundamentalists who invoke the notion of the 'ideal Muslim life', but it is not representative of Indian Muslim fundamentalism. It is simply one of the many streams—and by no means the dominant one. The more common strain is a hotchpotch of religiosity, cultural prejudices born out of ignorance, political opportunism, and a reaction to a sense of insecurity which may often be exaggerated but is not entirely without a basis.

There's a large tribe of lapsed Indian Muslim fundamentalists who want to put their past behind them and move on, but are too embarrassed to recant publicly. Some of their old self-righteousness—the hallmark of a good fundamentalist—prevents them from acknowledging openly that they got it wrong. Instead, they try to rationalize their old follies—blaming them on others or the circumstances. I heard excuses along the lines of 'But I was so young then…'; 'I was dragged into it by friends'; 'The circumstances then were such…'; 'It was a reaction…' etc.

Some of this has a whiff of how a lot of Muslims rationalized their decision to opt for Pakistan at the time of Partition, by citing peer and parental pressure or claiming they were victims of 'emotional blackmail'. It is also the case that many of the fundamentalists were actually simply opportunists, who spoke the language of fundamentalism or took fundamentalist positions because that was the language of the so-called Muslim 'leadership'. A classic example of the Muslims' fickle ideological convictions is Arif Mohammed Khan, a U.P. politician who has turned (political) party-hopping into a fine art. He started off as a rabble-rouser student activist at Aligarh Muslim University, joined the Congress and prospered until he fell out with it and joined the Janata Dal in a blaze of 'Hail Marys' from liberal Muslims—only to end up in the BJP!

Most Muslim fundamentalists are no different from their Hindu counterparts in that both see religion simply as continuation of politics by other means. The campaign to build a Ram temple on the site of the historic Babri Masjid in Ayodhya, and the counter Muslim campaign to protect it, was one such example of Hindu and Muslim fundamentalists deploying religion for political purposes. Like many otherwise decent and sensible Hindus who jumped on the Hindutva bandwagon when it seemed to be the only show in town, many Muslims often take fundamentalist positions simply because it seems like a good career move. The only difference is that while Hindu liberals stand up and challenge their lunatic fringe, Muslim liberals go AWOL for reasons that are discussed at length elsewhere in the book.

Ironically, it was a liberal Hindu leader who was to play a crucial role in weaning Muslims away from fundamentalism and mobilizing them around a broad secular 'social justice' plank. Under V.P. Singh, the Janata Dal offered a platform to young Muslims who had drifted towards fundamentalism because of a lack of a credible secular alternative. Singh's decision to implement the recommendations of the Mandal Commission (named after its chairman, B.P. Mandal, an MP) providing job reservations in public sector for the historically disadvantaged communities—Other Backward Classes (OBCs)—including Muslims, made him a hero and he was hailed as a 'messiah' by the community. He also went out of his way to bring in young secular Muslims into the political mainstream and picked them up to fight elections on his party's ticket, often in the face of opposition from his colleagues. In 1991, he offered Seema Mustafa, a liberal Muslim journalist, the Janata Dal ticket for a Lok Sabha seat from Domariaganj in U.P.—only for her to be disowned by the party later to accommodate a nominee of Ajit Singh, the leader of a rival faction.

Ms Mustafa has written about the profound impact Singh had on poor Muslims, especially in rural areas: 'He was a messiah for the rural folk, particularly the Muslims for whom he could do no wrong,' she writes in her book, *Azadi's Daughter: Journey of a Liberal Muslim,* contrasting Singh's agenda with the Congress Party's sectarian campaign which included 'hiring mullahs' to mobilise Muslim votes. Ultimately the Singh project fizzled out because of internal factionalism. As Ms Mustafa writes, he was 'an innocent, unable to handle the party or his colleagues'.

'The main problem was that whatever he promised was not implemented as the ground organisations were not under his control.' But his policies left a deep mark on the Muslim body-politic. 'He was the last of the secular leaders who tried to construct a non-sectarian platform for the Muslims in India and gave up power for this,' according to Krishna Ananth, a senior journalist, who closely followed Singh's campaign.

Even as he took care not to alienate the Muslim Right, and walked a tightrope on controversial issues, he saw the so-called 'Muslim Question' as part of a bigger fight for social justice for all weaker sections, irrespective of religion or caste. He was perhaps the only national leader of his generation who tried to restore to Muslims the dignity that they felt they had been stripped of under Congress patronage, when they were treated as a version of a necessary evil that had be to endured for votes.

'He gave us back our izzat,' said a Janata Dal activist who renounced fundamentalism under Singh's influence.

Like most reformed fundamentalists, he wouldn't go on record but was happy to tell what he grandly called his 'backstory'. And, as he told it, it didn't sound very different from those of others of his ilk. Let us call him Ahmed. Son of a local Congress activist, Ahmed had his own political ambitions as a student when he arrived at Aligarh Muslim University. It was the late 1970s, and the campus politics was controlled by a variety of fundamentalist groups under different names, backed by various political parties including the Congress. He discovered that the only way 'up' lay through them, and promptly joined a pro-Congress group. Soon he was leading protests, petitioning the vice-chancellor, meeting ministers, briefing the media. He had arrived.

'It was all very heady,' he admitted. But Ahmed's real break came during the infamous 1982 campaign in AMU against the eminent Marxist historian, Professor Irfan Habib, who was the head of the university's history department at the time and a vocal critic of fundamentalist elements on the campus. The agitation, which included physical attacks on him, was arguably one of the most sordid episodes in AMU's post-independence history and saw some of the murkiest aspects of Muslim politics play out in the open. The case dominated headlines for months. It revealed how a small clique of self-appointed Muslim 'leaders'—basically an alliance of Muslim Congress leaders and right-wing 'Islamic' groups on the campus—was able to hijack the country's premier Muslim institution, turning it into a personal fief by dispensing patronage and silencing critics such as Professor Habib.

Professor Habib was targeted for exposing how the university's admissions system was being abused by the ruling clique in the name of 'helping' Muslim students. He was particularly opposed to giving admissions to candidates who did not qualify or had a criminal background, and warned against compromising academic standards. (Indeed, his warning was to prove prophetic. As the word spread that the university was bending its admission rules to favour candidates of questionable merit, employers became wary of employing AMU graduates. One prominent Muslim company of U.P. went to the extent of publicly stating in a job advertisement: 'AMU graduates need not apply')

Even as his detractors were gunning for him, Professor Habib gave an interview to *The Indian Express* newspaper in which he spoke of the decline in university administration and, more controversially, pointed out that politically-connected goondas masquerading as students had taken over the campus.

The students' union, controlled by the right-wing Students' Islamic Movement of India (SIMI), which was to later get embroiled in terrorism, reacted with fury and unleashed a campaign of violent intimidation against Professor Habib and his supporters. Acting in concert with like-minded elements in the teachers' association, it pressured the vice-chancellor into issuing a charge-sheet to Professor Habib accusing him of 'misconduct' and 'maligning' the university.

The move, which was seen as a glaring example of how political parties were using student groups to advance their own agendas, caused outrage in liberal circles across the country, and sparked a nationwide debate on academic freedom and politicization of minority educational institutions.

Eminent historian Romila Thapar called the harassment of Professor Habib 'an absolute travesty of the very principles on which a university functions and a gross attack on the right of an academic to comment in public on the functioning of his institution'.

'Obviously the charge-sheet resulted from the pressure from local Muslim political groups whose real grouse against Professor Habib was that he was a man of liberal views, opposed to communalism in any form and was respected by those who had a secular and rational view of India's history and society,' she wrote in the People's Union of Civil Liberties (PUCL) bulletin.

As a young reporter, it was my first serious exposure to Muslim fundamentalism in action, and it left me deeply disturbed. Ahmed, meanwhile, became the media spokesman for what was to turn into a broader witch-hunt against suspected left-wing sympathisers. It propelled him on to the national stage and he was promptly embraced by the Congress. But he fell out with it over the Babri Masjid issue, joined the Janata Dal, and became personally close to Singh. After Singh's death he returned to the Congress but failed to regain his old importance.

Ahmed insists that he was never a 'religious extremist' and kept his distance from pro-sharia groups who, among other things, wanted to impose a dress code on Muslim women. His only 'sin', he says, was his ambition to become a political leader and admits to exploiting Muslim issues to achieve his goal.

Broadly, his is a typical portrait of an average Indian Muslim fundamentalist: a political operator using religious sensitivities to climb the greasy pole of 'Muslim leadership'. There were no missionaries or insurrectionists—only semi-literate rabble-rousers acting as proxies for larger sinister political forces. More toothless tigers than roaring lions they pretended to be. Sadly the media, and through it the wider society, bought into it their self-serving claims and turned them into larger-than-life characters.

6
Beyond Mullahs and Marxists

A Hindu friend once told me, even as he profusely apologized for his bluntness, that there was only one kind of Muslim—the fundamentalist kind. The idea of a 'liberal Muslim' was a 'misnomer' according to him. Such a person was first and foremost a liberal who also *happened* to be a Muslim because of the sheer accident of having born in a Muslim family.

'Their liberalism doesn't derive from Islam. It has nothing to do with their being Muslims. They are liberals *despite* being Muslims and not because they are Muslims. I have yet to meet a devout Muslim who doesn't have fundamentalist views. And mind you, I'm 70 plus and have known at least three generations of Muslims,' he said.

The notion that a practicing Muslim cannot be liberal has become conventional wisdom. And, to be honest, I have often found myself broadly agreeing with this view. Working in Delhi as a journalist until the late 1990s, I had a hard time finding sane, liberal voices, even in educated Muslim circles, on issues such as free speech, Muslim personal law, women's rights, and secularism. There were either the agnostic/atheist, mostly left-wing secular Muslims who felt almost embarrassed to be defined by their religious identity, or there were 'mainstream' devout Muslims—defensive, insular, intolerant and deeply suspicious of their secular peers contemptuously dismissing them either as communists or government stooges.

There is no doubt that all faith groups are divided along liberal/fundamentalist lines (Hindus, Sikhs and Christians have their own share of fundamentalist 'mullahs') but the divide among Muslims was particularly stark. It was as if these were not two sections of the same community but two separate communities with parallel and irreconcilable worldviews. The future looked bleak and, like many of my generation, I had written off any possibility of a change in the Muslim mindset in my lifetime.

But over the past decade it has all changed. Now there is a world beyond mullahs and Marxists, and the notion of a liberal Muslim does not sound so alien any more. It is amazing how much the Muslim mood has changed in recent years. Alas, my friend who had never known a practicing liberal Muslim is no more. I'm sure he would have been as pleased as I am to have been proved wrong in assuming that Muslims were beyond change. He would have enjoyed meeting the likes of Aqeel Ahmed, Meher Rahman, Nasir Zaidi, Saba Bashir, Arif Ahmed—to name just a few of the numerous young, educated and progressive Muslims I came across in the course of writing this book—who see no contradiction between religiosity and secularism, and whose faith in Islam does not stop them from being secular Indians. Many don't like the 'minority' tag which, they say, suggests as though they are on the fringes of Indian mainstream.

I routinely hear people lament that the Muslim mindset is still stuck in the 1980s and 1990s, mired in self-pity and a corrosive sense of victimhood with no room for introspection or debate. Apart from being extremely patronizing such a view is lazy stereotyping of a whole community, and betrays a huge amount of ignorance and prejudice. For the reality is quite different.

During my travels I found young Muslims vigorously debating the 'challenges' facing India's 170-million-strong Muslim community, and what should it do to haul itself out of the hole it is in. What particularly struck me was their courage to acknowledge what previous generations had doggedly refused to—namely, the community's own role in its destruction. For the first time there is a willingness to face up to the fact that many of the wounds the Muslims suffered, and for which they blamed others, were actually self-inflicted.

'Suicidal' is how young Muslims describe the tactics of successive post-partition generations. They believe they have been handed a legacy that speaks of their elders' profound failure to produce an enlightened and credible leadership. And they are angry.

'Muslims are architects of their own misery,' said Aamir Shahzad, a religiously devout post-graduate history student of Lucknow University, with barely suppressed fury. 'I hate to say it but my father and grandfather's generations have failed us. Their priorities have been wrong and we are paying for their mistakes. They allowed mullahs to become our spokesmen. And look where we are today.'

As an illustration of wrong priorities, many cite the fight that the community picked up over Babri Masjid. 'I am not saying that it was not an important issue but if we had made the same sort of noise over discrimination that Muslims face in everyday life, and in demanding good education and jobs, it would have made more sense,' argued Meraj Haider who runs a successful real-estate business in central U.P.

'Challenge' and 'priorities' were two terms I heard

frequently in my interactions with the Muslim youth. The community, I was told, must get out of its siege mentality; stop seeing enemies everywhere and start on a new slate. There is a deep generational divide, especially in the 18-25 age group. They believe that their parents' generation had been too 'defensive' about its Muslim identity and, for all its apparent secularism, tended to see India essentially as a 'Hindu' country and Muslims as a persecuted minority. Its perception of its Muslim identity was 'too negative', according to them.

I have some sympathy with this view though the theory, especially popular in the academia, that Muslims have always suffered from a deep existential 'identity crisis' as to who they were—'Muslims first or Indians first' (an agonized debate on this has raged for as long as I can remember) is vastly exaggerated, as I've argued in another chapter.

The identity issue has its roots in Partition. Not many Muslims will acknowledge this but let's be honest: it is a myth that every Muslim who chose to stay back in India was prompted by a sense of nationalism or was against the idea of Pakistan. Many stayed back simply because they found the sheer logistics of migration too daunting; others held back because of the fear of taking the plunge into an unknown and uncertain future; some tested the waters and decided that it was safer to hang back; and, indeed, quite a few—including some progressive Muslims—actually moved to Pakistan and returned when they discovered that it was not the promised land it was cracked up to be.

So the post-partition generation struggled with a massive historical baggage that, among other things, made it deeply conscious of its identity and its place in a Hindu-majority India—an 'infection' that it passed on to successive generations.

Muslims from that generation admit to suffering a 'Muslim complex', as some put it. But they attribute it to the political climate of the time.

'We were a product of our time. There was a climate of suspicion of Muslims because of Partition, and so on. There were communal riots every now and then, Urdu was being crushed because they said it was the language of Muslims…it was not easy to forget that you were a Muslim,' said Ahmed Qadri, who ran a library of Urdu books and journals in Old Delhi in the 1960s. He was forced to close down the library as Urdu publications and their readers declined, leaving him with few books to lend and even fewer customers to lend to.

'What happened to me happened because I was a Muslim… so how could I not be conscious of being a Muslim?' he asked.

Muslims of his generation say that the Hindu Right made it impossible for them to forget their minority status. They were regarded as 'lower orders who should know their place'.

For the younger generation of Muslims, on the other hand, Partition has no special resonance. It is something they read about in history books and feel no need to 'obsess about', as one young Muslim woman put it. Nor do they feel any special affinity towards Pakistan, which, if anything, they regard as a failed state—and an embarrassment. All this makes them less conflicted about their identity and minority status. They see themselves as any other Indian citizen except that they happen to be Muslims. They argue that Muslims are not the only minority group in India and there is no reason why they should put themselves in a special box.

But here's the paradox. Precisely because they don't suffer from the sort of identity crisis their parents did, they feel less inhibited about flaunting their 'Muslim-ness'. That explains the proliferation of beards and hijabs; and the rush to the masjid, a growing global trend among young Muslims. But they insist that this assertion of their 'Islamic identity' does not diminish their Indian-ness, which is what ultimately defines them. Allama Iqbal wrote, 'Hindi hain hum watan hai, Hindustan hamara.' And that pretty much sums up the modern Indian Muslim. Damn the beard.

7
The 'New' Muslim Woman

Faria Faruqi defies the popular stereotype of a middle-class Muslim woman struggling to breathe, or find her voice in a suffocating sharia-compliant atmosphere that is supposed to prevail in the Muslim community.

The 21-year-old mass communications student arrived at the Lucknow Press Club riding a massive motorcycle—a four-stroke Yamaha. Dressed in jeans and a plain top, she could pass for any modern young Indian woman. I told her jokingly that I was expecting someone in a hijab.

'What nonsense!' she retorted.

'Look, I don't like hijab and I don't think it is a great symbol of Muslim identity. But let me also tell you that every woman who wears a hijab or burqa is not a victim of oppression. There are lots of my friends who wear it of their own free will. It is none of my business to tell others what they should wear or not wear, just as I don't think it is any body's business to tell me what I should or should not wear. It is a free and democratic country and people should be free to dress the way they like. I am against any coercion and have no time for people who go about imposing dress codes.'

Faria had a liberal upbringing which she believes may have had something to do with the fact that her father is a progressive Urdu poet. But then she adds that her mother, though not very educated and a stay-at-home housewife, is even more liberal than her father in many ways.

'I was never discriminated against because I was a girl. In fact my brother always cribbed that I was a pampered child. They even bought me a motorcycle!'

Faria went to one of Lucknow's best schools and then to a college in Pune where she lived in a hostel, sharing a room with seven girls from different religious and cultural backgrounds.

Did she face any prejudice from her non-Muslim colleagues?

'No, I never felt left out or excluded. If there was any prejudice it was out of ignorance. In the end I became the resident mughlai chef! Even now, some of them write to me for recipes.'

Faria acknowledges that she is not a 'typical' Muslim girl and that a majority are 'conservative'. Her cousins, she says, lead much more restricted lives; and some of her elderly relations believe that her parents have allowed her too much freedom. Her own brother—the original owner of her motorbike—doesn't like her driving around on the streets of Lucknow and keeps telling her to dress more 'modestly'. But she makes it clear that she has no intention of compromising her independence.

The fact that she has refused to succumb to pressure is a sign that Muslim women are coming on their own. There may not yet be enough Farias but their number is growing. I witnessed a fascinating display of this 'fightback' at Aligarh Muslim University. While its reputation as a barometer of the Muslim mood may be exaggerated, it is a good place to get a sense of their thinking. AMU long ceased to be an opinion-setter but, given its cultural make-up, it remains a microcosm of broad Muslim trend. Contrary to its image of a north Indian Muslim ghetto it has a much more diverse base, drawing students and faculty from across India. One of its recent vice-chancellors P.K. Abdul Azis was from the south.

An outsider, just arrived in AMU, is likely to be misled by the sight of hijab and burqa-clad young women into believing that they are a conservative, backward-looking bunch. But most are highly independent, articulate and more liberal than many of their male peers. In fact, my research tells me that the average Indian Muslim woman today is generally more progressive than the average Muslim man. At AMU I found that almost on every issue of significance—from the question of identity and fundamentalism to how they saw their place in India—there were many more female liberal voices compared to men. In group discussions, men had a rough time as women robustly challenged their views. Their claims about Islamic dress code for women were greeted with furious accusations of self-serving selective interpretation of Islamic injunctions. At one such gathering, when a boy, Ahmar Afaq Ali, a law student said that it was compulsory in Islam for all women who regarded themselves as 'good Muslims' to wear hijab, he was bombarded with questions about his knowledge and understanding of Islam.

'Where did you read this?' retorted Saima Kareem, an undergraduate. 'All that Islam says is that women should dress modestly, but it doesn't lay down a dress code. It is men and the mullahs who keep telling us what to wear. Islam doesn't say that you stop being a good Muslim if you don't wear hijab or show off your so-called Muslim identity. I am no less a Muslim than those who wear hijab or burqa.'

There were a few hijab-wearing girls in the audience who insisted that they wore it of their own free will, but had a hard time convincing their non-hijabi colleagues.

Asma Sabzposh, a political science student, said there was constant pressure on women not only from their family but also from fellow male students to wear hijab. Most women who wore hijab did so under pressure, no matter how much they denied this, she claimed.

A girl, who didn't want to give her name, said that when she came to AMU from Delhi she felt 'very odd' as boys tried to 'indoctrinate' her. 'It was really very strange. They would come to you and start talking about Islam and the 'obligations' of a good Muslim, and how women must dress, etc.' she said.

It was not only in relation to their own personal freedoms that these girls so boldly and articulately challenged the boys. They took them on over a whole range of issues affecting Muslims—the 'real' reasons for their educational and economic backwardness; the persecution complex they suffered from; their understanding of secularism; and their future in India.

As someone who has reported AMU for some 30 years on and off, I noticed a massive change in the attitude of its women students. Not only are today's female students more progressive in their outlook, they are willing to speak their mind in public. Rewind to 20 years ago, and they would have raged privately, boiled with impotent anger but they would not have had the courage to speak up. Even by the standards of the timidity of Indian women generally, Muslim women have, traditionally, been even more timid because of a lack of education and the deeply conservative and oppressively patriarchal nature of the Muslim society. My mother, who was a communist party activist, was often frustrated as she struggled to organise Muslim women in Old Delhi. During elections they voted almost *en masse* according to the wishes of the men in their family. That was, of course, in the late 1950s and early 1960 sbut even until quite recently Muslim women enjoyed little independence.

Now there is a 'new' Indian Muslim woman on the scene. And yet, it seems, we have barely noticed her. That she can be found even in culturally conservative small towns—Aligarh, Meerut, Moradabad, Lucknow, Kanpur—shows that the change has spread beyond the big metros—and is real. This 'new' woman (18-30 age group) is politically aware, has strong independent views, and is not afraid to express them. And not only does she have aspirations, she is determined to pursue them.

I am struck by the range of professional careers that Muslim women are now opting for. Back in the late 1970s, when I entered journalism, the number of Muslim journalists in mainstream newspapers, irrespective of their gender, could be counted on one's fingertips. Muslim women journalists were even fewer—almost rare. Among my contemporaries I can think of only one: Seema Mustafa. Today, the mainstream media is awash with Muslim women—not just the print media, but also television and cinema. And more are coming. Media studies courses are full of young Muslim women. Other most-favoured occupations include law, corporate management, medicine, fashion design, and development, with many wanting to work in the voluntary sector or with international development agencies. How much aspirations have changed is reflected in the fact that these days very few young Muslim women profess interest in what used to be a traditional career path for them—teaching and nursing. They are now among the least favoured career options.

Over the past 20-25 years there has been an exponential expansion of higher education among Muslim women which, in turn, has boosted their aspirations. While once they were content to be school teachers, nurses, secretaries and receptionists, today they aspire to be corporate managers, entrepreneurs, civil servants, diplomats, lawyers—there is a self-belief that they are as good as men and there is no stopping them from achieving their ambitions. They have crossed the mental rubicon that kept them away from more demanding and high-profile careers.

The school dropout rate among Muslim women is still high and many still don't even get to go to school, but that does not negate the achievements of the past two decades. The time was when a Muslim woman was more likely to be uneducated than educated, but today the young Muslim woman you see on the street-corner is more likely to be on her way to university—a sign of the pace of change in the community despite the fundamentalists' bid to thwart it.

8
The Shah Bano Effect

It is often forgotten that the worst victims of Islamic fundamentalism are the Muslims themselves, especially women. Thanks to a narrow and selective interpretation of sharia laws, millions of Muslim women are condemned to living miserable lives: kept in purdah, discriminated against, denied property rights and vulnerable to arbitrary divorce and maintenance laws.

Hindi films such as 'Bazaar', in which a minor girl is sold by her parents to a rich Arab old enough to be her grandfather; and 'Nikaah', wherein an educated and supposedly liberal man divorces his wife in a fit of anger by simply pronouncing talaq three times, run uncomfortably close to the Muslim bone. They may seem melodramatic on the screen but the situations depicted in these films are real and would resonate with all Muslim women, even if personally they have not been through them. The power enjoyed by a Muslim man under a 'shotgun' divorce system that allows him to throw out his wife by uttering talaq thrice, is like the sword of Damocles permanently hanging over a woman's head. It has become an instrument of oppression in the hands of misogynist men and their mullah brethren, as illustrated by the infamously famous Shah Bano case which has come to be regarded as a milestone in Muslim women's search for social justice. It also sparked a fierce debate on the place of personal religious laws in a secular state.

Shah Bano was a 62-year-old mother of five from Indore, Madhya Pradesh. In 1978 she was divorced by her husband, an advocate who was already married to another woman. Denied maintenance and with no means to support herself and her children, she approached the courts for justice. A long legal battle ensued, going right up to the Supreme Court. Seven years later, in a landmark judgement in April 1985, the Supreme Court ordered the husband to pay her maintenance. It ruled that under Section 125 of Code of Criminal Procedure, which applies to every citizen of India regardless of caste, creed or religion, Shah Bano was entitled to basic maintenance, similar to alimony, with an upper limit of ₹500 a month.

The verdict was hailed not only as a victory for a destitute old woman in her search for justice, but also as a much-needed assertion of the supremacy of secular laws in a multicultural and multi-religious society. But the celebrations were to prove premature as fundamentalist Muslims kicked up a row and took to the streets claiming that the judgement encroached on their right to be governed by their own family laws, and was an attack on their religion. The word went out that it was a slippery slope towards imposing a uniform civil code on the Muslim community, and must be resisted. Conservative groups like the All-India Muslim Personal Law Board and prominent Muslim politicians weighed in with a noisy campaign to demand a new law to overturn the judgement.

The Congress government of Prime Minister Rajiv Gandhi, faced with street protests and warnings of a Muslim boycott of the party at the next election if it did not agree to their bidding, caved in. Using its absolute majority in Parliament, it brought in a legislation, the Muslim Women (Protection of

Rights on Divorce) Act, 1986, which reversed the Supreme Court verdict—a move which may have sounded smart at the time but was to prove disastrous both for Muslims and the Congress Party a few years later. But we will come to that in a bit.

Under the new law, the husband's liability to pay maintenance to his former wife was restricted to three months after the divorce—the so-called 'iddat' period that Muslim women observe after the death of their spouse or divorce from them during which time they are not supposed to marry again. After three months the onus of maintenance was shifted to her family or the wakf board. The law was seen as discriminatory to Muslim women as it excluded them from the purview of secular laws under which women of other faiths could seek basic maintenance.

The Statement of Objects and Reasons attached to the Act was explicit: 'Every application by a divorced woman under section 125...of the Code of Criminal Procedure, 1973, pending before a magistrate on the commencement of this Act shall, notwithstanding anything contained in that code...be disposed of by such magistrate in accordance with the provisions of this Act.'

Liberals were shocked by what they saw as blatant appeasement of Muslim fundamentalists in the name of protecting minority interests. It has since emerged how, before the new law was brought in, Shah Bano and her family were pressured into rejecting the Supreme Court judgement. According to her youngest son, Jameel Ahmed Khan, Rajiv Gandhi summoned her to Delhi and told her, 'The situation is very critical. We have to find a way.' He wanted her to publicly refuse the maintenance awarded by the Supreme Court—which she did.

After returning to Indore, she called a press conference to announce that she was forsaking the maintenance because it was against the Shariat.

'My mother was feted at public functions (by orthodox Muslims) and showered with titles like 'Deeni Bahan' (Righteous Sister) and 'Islami Behen' (Islamic Sister),' Jameel told *The Hindustan Times* in an interview (posted on its website on 11 November 2011).

Jameel's account needs to be detailed at length as it shows how an old and destitute woman was cynically exploited by clerics and fundamentalist Muslim leaders to keep themselves in business. Recalling the events following the Supreme Court judgement, he said: 'Former diplomat and prominent Muslim leader Syed Shahabuddin visited our house as did ulema (clergymen) from Indore and other cities, who told us that the verdict was against the Shariat. We didn't know much about it (Shariat provisions for maintenance, etc.) then...our mother was illiterate. Clergymen from India and abroad contacted us and told us that there had been a mistake and explained how things should be according to the Shariat.'

'Several people...offered money and even a job abroad (for refusing maintenance)...The pressure became such that I felt winning the case wasn't so good. It would've been better if we lost...Massive processions against the judgment were staged across the country. In Mumbai, traffic was held up for hours. Even in Indore there was a lakh-strong rally which passed in front of our house. Even if every rallyist threw a pebble each, our kuchha house would have crumbled. This creates terror.'

Jameel said that his mother, who died of brain hemorrhage in 1992, was exploited by clerics and politicians. The maintenance promised to her under the new law stopped after some time, and her final days were spent in penury.

'My mother was wronged, gravely wronged. My mother was a simple, purdah-observing woman. Being divorced at such a late age (60, by most accounts), the publicity, paper-baazi... she was very ashamed of all this. She didn't say much but kept stewing over it,' said Jameel.

He still lives in the same modest house in Indore where his mother suffered and died. Nobody offers him money or a job anymore because he is of no political use to them now.

As in life, so in politics there are no free lunches, and for Muslims the bill for the Shah Bano lunch arrived even before they had finished celebrating their 'victory'. The price they had to pay was so heavy that, more than two decades later, the community is still reeling from it. The price was Babri Masjid. There's a widely-held belief that the masjid, which was demolished by a mob of Hindu fanatics in 1992, would have still been standing but for the way Muslims handled the Shah Bano affair.

This is what happened.

After winning plaudits from Muslim fundamentalists for overturning the Supreme Court verdict in the Bano case, the Rajiv Gandhi Government turned to appease Hindu fundamentalists who had launched a massive nationwide agitation for the opening of the locks of the Ramjanam Bhoomi-Babri Masjid complex, which was sealed on court orders in 1949 because of a historical dispute over competing Hindu-Muslim claims. In the same month that it reversed the Shah Bano judgement, the government allowed the locks of the Masjid complex to be removed to allow Hindu worshippers access to the part of the mosque which they regard as the exact spot where Ram was born. Until then, only a priest was permitted to perform puja once a year for the idols installed there in 1949.

Suddenly, hundreds and thousands of Hindu devotees—mostly Trishul-wielding, saffron-robed activists of the Hindu Vishwa Parishad and Bajrang Dal—descended on Ayodhya to have a 'darshan' of 'Ram Lalla', giving a big momentum to the VHP's campaign for building a Ram Temple on the disputed site. Muslim groups responded by launching their own campaign to 'protect' the mosque under the guidance of the hastily-formed Babri Masjid Action Committee, with many of the same leaders who had led the protest against the Shah Bano judgement in starring roles. Even as communal tension was rising, spreading beyond Ayodhya, the government compounded the situation by allowing the VHP to perform a shilanyas (stone-laying ceremony) for a proposed Ram Temple at a spot close to the disputed site in November 1989, in what was seen as part of the Congress Party's electoral strategy to soften Hindu voters ahead of a general election.

This gave further headwind to the BJP-VHP's Ram Temple campaign and, in September 1990, L.K. Advani embarked on his famous 10,000 km cross-country Rath yatra, setting in train a chain of events that two years later culminated in the demolition of Babri Majsid. Rest is history. What seemed like a clever strategy at the time—keeping both Hindu and Muslim fundamentalists happy, even at the risk of tearing apart the country's secular fabric—boomeranged on the Congress. Post-Babri Masjid, the party was abandoned by Muslims *en masse*. The Hindus, who had already deserted it accusing it of pseudo-secularism and minority appeasement, never returned in sufficient numbers for it to ever form a government on its own since then.

For the Muslim community, the Shah Bano affair remains a huge embarrassment, and even many conservative Muslims admit they messed up.

But, on the positive side, it radicalized the Muslim women who have not only become more aware of their rights but are more willing to stand up for them. It is unlikely that they will allow another Shah Bano to happen.

A good example of the new awakening among Muslim women is the Imraana rape case. Imraana, a 28-year-old mother of five from Muzaffarnagar, Uttar Pradesh, was raped by her father-in-law Ali Mohammad on 6 June 2005. But instead of punishing the rapist, a local Muslim panchayat declared it a case of adultery on the part of Imraana and ruled that her marriage to her husband Nur Ilahi stood null and void. She was now to treat him as her son. A fatwa issued by Darul Uloom, Deoband, endorsed the ruling. There was a huge nationwide uproar. Imraana stood her ground and, defying the panchayat's ruling and Darul Uloom's shocking fatwa, continued to live with her husband who fully supported her. As protests grew, the mood started to change. Darul Uloom hastily withdrew the fatwa claiming it had never issued it in the first place. Meanwhile, the National Commission for Women, which had been slow to react, finally acted and sought the arrest and prosecution of the rapist father-in-law. He was arrested, tried and sentenced to 10 years' imprisonment on 19 October 2006. He was also directed to pay Imrana a fine of ₹8,000, which apparently he never did.

The reaction to the Imraana row from the wider civil society, as well as Muslim women, was in refreshing contrast to the Shah Bano case. Such was the pressure from conservative groups at the time that even liberal Muslim women were reluctant to come out publicly in support of Shah Bano. But, ultimately, they saw through the conspiracy to keep them down on the pretext of protecting the Muslim way of life; and, confronted with the plight of Imraana (another poor Muslim woman being persecuted in the name of religion), they decided that enough was enough.

Today, wiser by experience and having become more conscious of their rights, many more Muslim women are prepared to speak out against discriminatory sharia laws. Social activists who work with Muslim women say they have become more 'assertive' in challenging old dogmas, and pressing for more gender-just laws. And it is not just rhetoric. They are taking concrete steps and have already come up with an alternative 'ideal nikaahnama' designed to protect the rights of a divorced woman. Self-important guardians of Muslim personal law, such as the All India Muslim Personal Law Board, are under increasing pressure to introduce reforms based on a more progressive interpretation of sharia laws.

'For a new beginning, and to create a new chapter in the history of the community, Muslim women have in recent years taken the lead and made some remarkable contribution by moving the debate on law reform to the next level. The formulation of an ideal nikaahnama and an initiative in drafting an alternative gender-just laws are some key advances made by Muslim women. Muslim women, in recent years, have also formed associations and organizations to address their concerns and highlight the larger issues of the community, thus taking on its leadership,' write Noorjehan Safia Niaz, a founder-member of the Mumbai-based Bharatiya Muslim Mahila Andolan, and J.S. Apte, writer on development issues, in a joint paper published in the book *Lives of Muslims in India*.

Greater social awareness and increased support from the wider civil society means that Muslim women are no longer prepared to suffer silently in unhappy marriages. Niaz and Apte cite figures to show that while earlier Muslim women in unhappy marriages waited 'for at least 5-6 years or sometimes even ten years before they walked out of a marriage, now the time gap has reduced to a year or even less.'

However, there is still a long way to go, given the deeply-entrenched male attitudes and the continuing stranglehold of the mullahs. Besides, too many Muslim women are still uneducated, unaware of their rights and wholly economically dependent on men. Ultimately, Muslim women's fight for fairer family laws is linked to their wider, bigger struggle for social and economic emancipation. Real empowerment will come through education and economic independence. It is only when they don't have to worry where their next meal will come from that they will be able to stand up to male bullying.

What the Shah Bano case crucially did was to open up the debate on reforming the Muslim Personal Law, and to separate the issue of what Muslims can do to change their own laws from that of imposing a Common Civil Code. Until then, any call for reform was misconstrued by conservative Muslims as a trick to smuggle in a uniform civil code. It was also the case that historically the demand came mostly from a left-wing liberal Muslim elite who secretly favoured a uniform secular law for everyone. For the first time, it is coming from *within* the community—with women themselves leading the charge. So the pressure this time is real—and one that even the most dyed-in-the-wool fundamentalist would find hard to fob off with the bogey of the threat to Islam.

9
Shahi Imam Who?

Mention the word 'Muslim' and it evokes images of a community which is completely out of touch with the modern world, stuck in a time-warp; and defensive and groaning under the weight of self-pity and a persecution complex. The truth though is that such a perception is way out of date—an indication of how much the wider Indian community is ignorant about the new Muslim mood. Yes, there was a time when the above image was an accurate description of Indian Muslims. I remember how the dinner-table talk in most Muslim homes used to turn on the perceived persecution of Muslims. It was all about anti-Muslim prejudice and discrimination; and what others were doing to Muslims rather than what Muslims were doing to themselves. There was much hand-wringing about Hindu communalism laced with anger against secular parties such as the Congress, which many Muslims believed (still do) simply pretended to be secular in order to get their votes. Listening to that sort of talk was like listening to death-row prisoners. But, no more. The conversation today is more about the 'enemy within', about looking ahead and moving forward, and about what Muslims themselves can do to make the community stand on its own feet and face the challenges of the 21st century.

Young Muslims are seeking a new future which will not be

clouded by what happened in the past. 'To hell with Ayodhya and BJP, let's get on with our lives', is a common refrain. 'Mullahs' and (Muslim) politicians are the most hated class on India's Muslim streets today. For much of the past 60 years or so this class thrived by acting as middlemen for the Congress and its secular variants/rivals, in a deal whereby they delivered Muslim votes to their benefactors in return for political patronage. But now it looks like their game is finally up. There is no doubt that they are far too deeply entrenched to be wished away overnight, and a significant majority of Muslims remains vulnerable. But the pressure on them is growing with their self-styled 'ownership' of the community under serious threat, as the community is starting to realize the folly of putting its fate in their hands and allowing itself to become a vote bank. The new mood is determinedly against being taken for granted.

According to journalist and commentator Seema Chishti, the 'atomisation' of the Muslim vote and indeed the Muslim identity is the biggest story of the new awakening sweeping through India's Muslim community.

'Increasingly, Muslims are now acting as individuals than as a community. There is no such thing as a 'Muslim vote' any more—that's the biggest change that has happened. Not only have they realized the power of their vote, they have also become more pragmatic and tactical. In the Godhara (Gujarat) 2010 municipal elections some Muslims even voted for the BJP,' she says.

This change in the community's political attitude reflects a new hard-headed survival strategy in contrast to its emotional responses in the past. The era when the Shahi Imam of Delhi's Jama Masjid could use religion to mobilise Muslims across the country or set the national 'Muslim agenda' is over. Now even local Muslims don't take him seriously, choosing instead to act on their own instincts as to what is best for them.

'Mullahs have had their day, and they are conscious of their dwindling hold on the community,' says Ms Chishti.

She believes that one contributory factor in the 'atomisation' of the Muslim community is the nature of modern living itself. It has made lives so 'intertwined' that nobody, however obsessed with their religious or cultural identity, can stand apart without being completely isolated and cut off from the rest of the society. In an increasingly inter-dependent era, public transactions take place not between communities but between individuals rendering the idea of sectarian identities irrelevant, at least in the market place.

The collapse of Pakistan, she says, has also helped as Indian Muslims have now stopped looking across the border in search of a 'pan-Islamic' identity.

But I would be cautious in linking the events in Pakistan to the changed psyche of Indian Muslims because there is no evidence for it. For all the talk of Indian Muslims' so-called 'Pakistan connection' the fact is that they never took their 'line' from Pakistan. I firmly believe that the new self-awakening among Indian Muslims—their answer to the 'Arab Spring'—is entirely home-made and driven by the community's own belated realisation of its past mistakes. It is important to remember that the change is being driven by young Muslims whose Pakistan connection is almost non-existent. There is a new post-partition generation on both sides and neither relates to the other in the way their ancestors did, the old family ties having become weakened with the passing away of the older generation.

In any case, the notion of a pan-Islamic identity was always a myth. Arab Muslims, for example, despise South Asian Muslims and regard them as inferior except, of course, when they need them to propagate their fundamentalist version of Islam through funding Wahhabi-inspired madrassas. Returning to Pakistan, while it is true that some Indian Muslims nursed a kindred feeling towards a country invented in the name of Islam, the overwhelming majority was never enamoured with it. Here, I will let my Hindu Right friends into a little secret. They will be disappointed to know that there has never been any love lost between Indian Muslims and their co-religionists across the border. Their relations have been marked by a simmering mutual resentment and rivalry. Many Pakistanis regard Indian Muslims as traitors to the 'cause'. The latter tend to return the compliment by labelling Pakistanis as fundamentalists.

But that is another story; best left for another time.

Meanwhile, it is significant that the Indian Muslim awakening, or the churning that is going on in the community, is happening at all considering that Muslims had been written off as being incapable of self-introspection. It is good to see that after such deep slumber and decades of self-pity, sloth and indifference, they have been jolted into action and taken stock of their priorities. The wait for Godot may not be over, but at last there are voices insisting on a radical, historical break with the self-destructive and counter-productive approach of the past. This would mean moving away from politically-instigated sectarian agendas of the past to concentrate on a survival strategy firmly focused on the community's own interests and real issues such as education and jobs. Muslims recognise that they will need to stop blaming others and using anti-Muslim prejudice to cover-up their inadequacies. There is a new sense of urgency; and though more palpable among young Muslims, it is not confined to them alone.

'The Muslim Street is buzzing,' says Ms Chishti, contrasting it with the defeatist, sullen mood of yesteryears.

I heard plenty of *mea culpas* from older Muslims—how they got it wrong though these often came with the rider that the times were different then ('Jaba hawa alag thee').

But let's pause here. For it is easy to get carried away. Yes, the 'hawa' smells different; and yes, there is fighting talk about reform and 'setting the house in order'. Moreover, for the first time there is a new optimism that is hard to escape. But in large sections of the community old ways of thinking and doing things remain deeply entrenched, and not just among the older generation. A worryingly large number of young Muslims, notably men, still speak the language of the 1970s and 1980s; and large swathes of the community continue to behave as a persecuted group.

The big change, however, is that it is no longer the dominant trend. The voices of fundamentalism and reaction are facing increasing isolation—and are struggling. The agenda-setters of not-so-long-ago are in retreat. Traditional centres of Islamic learning such as Darul Uloom, Deoband and Darul Uloom Nadwa, regarded as heartlands of Muslim conservatism, are under intense pressure to reform. Deoband had a first taste of this new 'hawa' in January 2011 when for the first time in its 200-year history, a reforming 'outsider'—Maulana Ghulam Mohammed Vastanavi—a progressive Gujarati Islamic scholar with an MBA degree to boot, and a well-known educationist—was elected as its new Mohtamim or vice-chancellor.

The election of 60-year-old Vastanavi—widely recognised as the progressive face of Islamic clergy—represented not only a generational shift in Deoband (his predecessor Maulana Marghoob ur Rehman was 20 years older than him) but it was also seen as a signal for change in an institution stuck in a time-warp.

Shahid Siddiqui, a liberal politician and editor of Urdu newspaper *Nai Duniya*, hailed his election as 'a revolution' akin to the Arab spring.

'Let not people say, there goes the Maulvi who is a terrorist. Let them say, there goes the Maulvi who is a doctor, a heart-surgeon,' he said at a gathering of Muslim clerics, students and leaders held at Delhi's Ghalib Academy on February 21, 2011 *(The Hindu)*. Others described him as a 'beacon of hope' for Deoband.

'As a graduate from Darul Uloom Deoband, I know that students there are thirsting for democracy, reform and modern education. Vastanavi is their hope, and if he is removed, it will send out a bad signal,' said Maqsood ul Hasan Qasmi, president of the Imam Council of India, referring to attempts by a deeply-entrenched cabal of status quoists to remove him. (Vidya Subrahmaniam, *The Hindu*, 3 March 2011).

But within weeks of landing the job, Vastanavi ran into trouble with the 'old school', long used to calling the shots. It now saw him as a threat to their own interests. Attempts were made to cast Vastanavi as an 'outsider'—a rich Gujarati 'sahukar' (trader) who would not 'fit in' with Deoband's traditions. And while this was going on, it emerged that Vastanavi had made a speech in which he urged Muslims of Gujarat to patch up with the Modi administration. He claimed that like other communities Gujarati Muslims too had benefited from the state's economic progress, and that they should look beyond the 2002 riots. This was god-send for his critics who promptly seized on his remarks to accuse him of being an 'apologist' for Narendra Modi and of 'betraying' his own community. The right-wing Urdu press weighed in with sensational coverage to whip up emotions against Vastanavi.

Despite his repeated clarifications that his comments did not mean that he endorsed Mr Modi or condoned his administraton's actions during the riots, he was sacked after a kangaroo court, in the form of an inquiry committee appointed by Majlis-e-Shoora, the powerful governing body of the institution packed with status quoists, declared him guilty of giving a 'clean chit' to Mr Modi.

An understandably furious Vastanavi called his sacking a 'politically motivated move' and warned against attempts by an insular cabal to destroy South Asia's most famous seminary in the name of 'protecting' it from 'outsiders'.

'Those who earn their bread by politicking did not want me to stay (in Deoband). They did not allow me to do any work during my seven-month stint here. But they must understand that Darul Uloom is not the heirloom of any particular family.'

His message to the plotters was that he would not be cowed.

'Vastanvi koyi aira ghaira nahin hai (Vastanvi is not a pushover). I have multiple institutes and madrasas to run...I will continue to contribute to the society.'

It will be tempting to read this episode as a sign of the mullahs' continuing stranglehold on the Muslim community and its institutions—and the community's refusal to change. But that will be only partially true. For me, it was the Muslim reaction to Vastanavi's arbitrary dismissal that was more important in terms of the message it sent out to the fundamentalist groups.

Whereas once such a move would have gone unchallenged, this time the community at large reacted with fury. Vastanavi's termination was widely and publicly condemned. A group of

Deoband students called the Shoora's decision 'theological terror' and a victory for 'rudiwadi' (obscurantist) elements. Both the election of Vastanavi and the debate sparked by his controversial sacking reflect a yearning for change that is only likely to grow in the face of attempts to repress it. Pro-reform Deobandi say the resistance from the so-called 'traditionalists' is simply a 'holding operation'.

'The time is not on their side. The countdown has begun and they know it,' one reformist said optimistically.

Observers with inside knowledge of Deoband's internal politics say that Vastanavi was a 'casualty' of a 'turf war' between the warring factions of the Jamiat Ulamai-Hind (JUH), one of the country's most influential Muslim groups which has historically controlled Deoband through its chief, Maulana Sayed Asad Madani. After his death in 2006, his son Mahmood Madani, a Rajya Sabha MP from Uttar Pradesh and his uncle, Arshad Madani, fell out. Apparently, Vastanavi's appointment had the blessings of Mahmood Madani but was opposed by his uncle, who wanted the post for himself. Finally, the two were persuaded to patch up and a compromise candidate Maulana Abul Qasim Nomani was appointed to replace Vastanavi.

At Darul Uloom, Nadwa, Lucknow, I witnessed a heated exchange between three local educated young Muslims (a businessman, a banker, and a journalist) and a Nadwa official who dismissed any criticism of Muslims as biased and product of anti-Muslim prejudice. Maulana Obaidul Rahman, who runs Nadwa's media wing, is an articulate, well-travelled, well-informed young man, fluent in English, author of several books and a regular contributor to newspapers. I must confess that it says something about my own prejudice about such institutions that I was slightly surprised to find someone so urbane in a place swarming with long beards, skullcaps and hijabs, and reeking of insularity. But my delight was to prove shortlived. As we got talking, he sounded typically like a stick-in-the-mud Muslim to whom self-introspection seemed like an alien concept. He trotted out the usual arguments: how Muslims were persecuted, misunderstood, smeared and discriminated against. In short, Muslims were always right, others always wrong.

However, when I narrated my Nadwa experience to others, I was told that the fact that a senior figure agreed to talk to me at all and was willing to be drawn into a debate was itself 'progress' and a sign of openness. Apparently it used to be such a 'closed shop' that—in the words of one person with previous links to Nadwa—they wouldn't even 'give outsiders the time of the day' let alone debate inconvenient issues.

'It is news to me that they have become so media savvy. So, things are changing,' he said.

One optimistic view is that even in those parts of the Muslim community or institutions where change is not visible, there has been no visible regression either. Which itself is a hopeful sign. This reminded me of what the late prime minister Mr Narasimha Rao famously said, when attacked for lack of decision-making in his government: Not taking a decision, he retorted, was also a decision!

So, not regressing is also progress.

10
A Legacy of Ayodhya

I grew up hearing and reading about Indian Muslims' supposed 'identity crisis' but was never quite able to grasp what it really meant. If it meant that Muslims found themselves torn between their religious and national identities, I didn't find any evidence of it either in my own case or among other Muslims. To me it always seemed like a spurious debate whipped up mostly by the Hindu Right, with the aim of raising doubts about the Muslim community's 'Indian-ness'. Soon, even secularists bought into it and it became fashionable to portray Muslims as being outside the 'national mainstream'. It was said that they did not want to 'integrate' with the wider Indian national mainstream because they regarded themselves as Muslims first and Indians later.

The tactics of the Muslim Right did not help. By constantly harping on a narrow sectarian agenda in which demands for Muslim Personal Law, minority status for Muslim institutions, and opening up locks of abandoned mosques took precedence over the community's secular needs—jobs, education and housing—it reinforced the perception of a community obsessed with its religious identity. Muslims also gave the impression of spectacularly failing the famous 'cricket loyalty test' when a fanatic Muslim fringe insisted on cheering Pakistan in sporting events against India. Yet, the issue of the identity crisis that Muslims supposedly suffered from remained at best an academic exercise. Until, Ayodhya happened.

It was in the aftermath of the forcible demolition of Babri Masjid by Hindu zealots on 6 December 1992—an act designed to show who was the boss in 'secular' India—that for the first time Muslims actually became conscious of their religious identity. In the months leading to that show of majoritarian muscle, the nation was swept by a wave of a particularly virulent form of Hindu nationalism, not witnessed since the Partition. There is only one word to describe the mood: ugly. Muslims were publicly harassed. The air was awash with slogans calling them 'Babar ki Aulad' and asserting the Hindu 'ownership' of India where Muslims ('descendants' of Moghul conquerors) were simply interlopers.

This was an India that was new to me. I will never forget the sense of isolation I felt when, on the day of the demolition, I went to attend an official briefing in New Delhi's Shastri Bhavan, which housed the Government of India's information wing. There was not a single person in that crowded room, overflowing with reporters and TV crews, who was not quietly triumphal. What should have been a moment of reflection (where was India headed? Had secularism lost the fight?) was instead marked by a barely concealed celebration of the fact that finally Muslims had been shown their place.

Next day I wrote a somewhat emotional article in *The Hindu* ('A Noble Dream Shattered') lamenting the death of secularism in India, and arguing how it had made the task of secular Muslims in combating Muslim fundamentalism more difficult. I also suggested that it had implications for other minority groups in India whose faith in the Indian state's capacity—indeed willingness—to uphold its secular professions had been rudely shaken.

I wrote: 'To say that the faith in a professed secular state's capacity and its political will to uphold the constitution is rudely shaken may be construed as a knee-jerk reaction, but there is no doubt that it would take a long time to restore the sense of confidence not just among the Muslims but minorities across the board. The task of liberal Muslims in the circumstances becomes much more difficult, caught up as they are between their community's intolerance and Hindu communalism. Next time around, their plea for reason is likely to carry far less conviction with the Muslim hotheads.'

In his book, *Legacy of a Divided Nation: India's Muslims from Independence to Ayodhya* (Westview Press 1997), historian Mushirul Hasan noted that in 'the ebb and flow of Hindu-Muslim relations, the vandalism at Ayodhya represented a regressive current, in which brazen intimidation was seen to triumph in the full view of the state machinery'.

The Ayodhya episode and the anti-Muslim hysteria that it unleashed had a profound effect on every Muslim irrespective of their stand on the merits of mandir-masjid dispute. It shook up the Muslims of every persuasion (including those who had never regarded themselves as Muslims except in name) and, for the first time, we saw a historically divided community come together—as families do in times of grief—to ponder the implications of what had happened in Ayodhya.

'Is it the end of the road for Indian secularism? Will secular India survive?' was the question on every secular Indian's lips. Leading scholars debated the issue in a widely acclaimed book *'Will Secular India Survive?'* They raised questions about Muslim identity and reflected on Muslim fears that under Hindutva—the official ideology of militant Hindu nationalists—their constitutionally guaranteed rights may be gradually eroded, and they could be reduced to second-class citizens for all practical purposes.

Years later I heard actor Shabana Azmi—daughter of diehard Communist activists who grew up in a godless commune—recall how it had been the 'most traumatic' experience of her life. 'Until then, I had taken my composite culture for granted but, for the first time, I was made conscious that I was not simply another Indian citizen but a Muslim. I couldn't believe this was happening. My multicultural world was shattered with the Shiva Sena wanting proof of my loyalty,' she said.

Speaking at Nehru Centre in London in the summer of 2009, Ms Azmi explained her transformation from being simply a 'cultural' Muslim with a taste for 'biryani' and Urdu poetry into someone who was now acutely conscious of her Muslim identity and insisted on flaunting it.

'I'm an actor, I'm a Muslim, I'm a social activist...,' is how she described herself in a short film on her life and work.

Reporting her remarks in The Hindu (8 May2009) I wrote: 'Ms Azmi's stress on her religious identity would seem strange to anyone familiar with her background— daughter of diehard Communist activists; childhood spent in a godless commune; and married, by choice, to a progressive, non-practicing poet and film-maker. Had I misheard? Was she quoted out of context? Odd though her remark might have sounded, I would be lying if I said I was surprised. For this is what post-Ayodhya and post-9/11 climate has done: made even notional and accidental Muslims conscious of their religion. I know Muslims who once despaired of religious tags but are now increasingly tending to go the Shabana Azmi way, though, in India, the situation is not yet as dire as in the West where Muslims are going to absurd lengths to assert their Islamic identity... There was little new in what Ms Azmi said but it was obvious that she felt hurt; and her new-found obsession with her Muslim identity shows what the anti-Muslim hysteria has done even to the moderate Muslim mind... One doesn't necessarily have to swallow the Muslim protestations of innocence and victimhood (a lot of their difficulties are of their own making) to understand why they feel the way they do, but a crude display of religious identity is still hard to justify.'

There was not a single Muslim—old, young, man, woman, progressive, conservative, fundamentalist, secular—who was not scarred by what happened on 6 December 1992. It has become part of the collective Muslim memory of humiliation. Muslims were shaken by the Hindu reaction which tended to equate India with Hindus suggesting that by virtue of being Hindus they had first claim on it. To their shock and horror, they found that such attitudes were no longer confined to the usual Hindutva suspects—Bajrang Dal, the Hindu Vishwa Parishad and the BJP—but had come the standard Hindu line. Young Muslims recall how it affected them as schoolchildren. Their Hindu classmates started behaving 'strangely' and would refer to them as 'you Muslims'. Some asked them why were Muslims not allowing Hindus to build a temple in their 'own land'.

'Obviously, it was something they had heard at home and were bringing to the school,' one young lecturer who was in his teens at the time told me.

Saba Mahmood Bashir, a left-wing Delhi-based academic from Allahabad, said she was eleven and had until then no awareness of the Hindu-Muslim divide.

'We were only two Muslim girls in a class of 40 and we noticed a visible change in the attitude of our Hindu classmates.

They would start talking about going for kar seva at Ayodhya. So it suddenly hit us that we were Muslims. Ayodhya certainly deepened my Muslim identity,' she said.

In what Muslims saw as a deliberate provocation, their Hindu neigbhours distributed 'laddoos' to celebrate the demolition of Babri Masjid, which had been portrayed as a symbol of Muslim 'conquest'.

The post-Partition India had never been so communally polarised before. There was a sense that the clock had been turned back to 1947. But if it was a wake-up call for secular India, it was also a moment of reckoning for Muslims. The demolition of the masjid was a belligerent assertion of Hindu supremacy, a way of telling the Muslims where they 'belonged'. Many Muslims say it was actually a blessing in disguise for the community as it shook it out of its complacency and forced it to stand on its own feet.

The current 'new' mood is widely traced back to those dark days when Muslims found themselves staring at a deeply uncertain future and confronted with some inconvenient questions about their priorities. And for once, sensibly, they came to the view that the way forward lay not in relying on political patronage or looking up to the state for 'minority' handouts but in setting their own house in order. This meant that they must stop being 'led' by self-styled leaders, decide for themselves what was in their own interest (if voting BJP in special circumstances was in their interest, vote BJP), put their head down and focus on their economic and educational development. A whole new generation of Muslims—those who were very young at the time of the Ayodhya or born later—grew up determined not to repeat the mistakes of its predecessors. And it is this generation that represents India's 'Muslim spring'.

Another defining moment for Muslims, not just in India but worldwide, was 9/11, and the Muslim reaction was, well, reactionary. In a mindless copycat imitation of what Muslims were doing in the West, young Indian Muslims started growing beards and wearing hijabs, the so-called symbols of Islamic identity, though, in fact, these have no religious sanction. It was rather a perverse assertion of identity and a complete misreading of the situation of Muslims in the West. I came across a lot of rationalization. Some drew parallels with the black American movement to 'reclaim' black identity ('black is beautiful') as a reaction to intense racial prejudice.

'There's a negative image of Muslims out there. We want to correct that. We're saying that we are proud to be Muslims and in case you think every Muslim in a beard is a terrorist, look at us: we're practicing Muslims, we've beards but we're not terrorists. We're proud Indians and proud Muslims,' said Nasir Zaidi, a successful young Delhi businessman, who grew a beard four years ago.

Some said that the post-9/11 Islamophobia made them more curious about Islam, and as they dipped into it they were drawn by its 'simplicity' and 'universal spiritual values'.

'I grew up as a cultural Muslim who had a Muslim name and celebrated Muslim festivals but, after 9/11, I started reading about Islam to find out whether what its critics were saying about it was true. I was fascinated by its simplicity, its belief in equality, non-violence and its stress on education. I found that it was the simplest religion to practice,' said Ghayasuddin Haider, a doctor.

Even those who don't advertise Islamic 'symbols' say they feel strongly about their Muslim identity and want to express it in different ways. Mehar Rehman, a young Delhi-based development activist, said she wanted others to know that she was a Muslim.

'We need to tell them that all Muslims are not beards and burqas. I don't want others to define or caricature my identity. At international conferences abroad, especially in the West, I make a conscious effort to tell people that I'm a Muslim. I want them to know that they have stereotyped Muslims. I don't fit their stereotype,' she said.

She doesn't wear hijab but says she has no problem with those who do so voluntarily, and so long as it doesn't come in the way of their professional life. She insists that her awareness of her Muslim identity doesn't detract from her identity as an Indian, and that she is as much a proud Indian as a proud Muslim. Nor does her 'Muslim-ness' make her blind to the faults of her own community. Meher comes from a family of liberal academics and is part of a growing movement of Muslim youth which wants to bring change to the community and help transform the public perception about Muslims. She has founded the Taameer India Foundation to promote educational and health issues among women.

'I am an audacious optimist and I am sure we will win,' she says.

Some, however, overdo the identity bit. I was told about a student of Delhi's Stephen's College who insisted on wearing a burqa to college. Her brother, Irfan Khalid, who runs an advertising agency, said there was no family pressure on her to wear a burqa and that it was entirely her own decision. In highlighting his sister's case Khalid was, of course, trying to debunk the notion that (1) Muslim women were held back from education; (2) that all those who wore burqa did so under compulsion; and (3) that burqa equalled backwardness.

Like other minorities, Muslims have fallen into what sociologists call the 'identity trap', and how others see them has become an obsession. Being proud of one's Muslim identity does not mean hanging a board around one's neck saying: 'Look here I am, a Muslim, and I am proud of it.' It has echoes of the Hindutva slogan of 'Garv se kaho hum Hindu hain' ('Say with pride that I am a Hindu'). Proclaiming pride in identity has unsavoury historical connotations. Nazis insisted they were proud of their identity; Italian fascists flaunted their identity with pride; Stalinists were proud to be Stalinists.

The idea that proclaiming pride in your identity from rooftops would change others' perceptions of who they think you are, is fundamentally flawed. And let's remember the stark truth that invariably there's a basis for perceptions, even if often tenuous. Don't forget that bearded Muslim suicide bombers committed acts of terrorism in the name of Islam. There's also the fact that, traditionally, beards and burqas have represented a regressive strain among Indian Muslims. Muslims, almost without exception, fail to confront the truth in their emotional battle for identity. In *Legacy of a Divided Nation* Mushirul Hasan argued that being a Muslim is just one of several competing identities for any individual; that there has never been a homogeneous 'Muslim India', whether in doctrine, custom, language or political loyalty; and that to make the most of their potential, Muslims should hold firmly to the idea of a society committed to social justice and freedom.

Another prominent historian, Gyanendra Pandey, has traced the Muslim identity question to the post-Partition Hindu distrust of Muslims who had decided to stay back in India, and constituted a significant section of its population.

'But the question remained: can a Muslim really be an

Indian? This is one of the enduring legacies of Partition in India, and it has more than a little to do with the way in which Indian nationalism and the Indian state have gone about the task of managing 'difference' from that day to this,' he writes in *Can a Muslim Be an Indian (Cambridge University Press 1999)*. That legacy of Partition has taken on a sharper edge in the aftermath of Ayodhya and 9/11.

11
The Rushdie Test

If there were a 'Rushdie test' of tolerance to determine people's capacity to tolerate a dissenting or controversial viewpoint, a majority of Indian Muslims would fail it. That may also be the case with other faith groups—Hindus, Sikhs and Christians—but let's stick to Muslims because this book is about them. The worldwide Muslim reaction to Salman Rushdie's 1988 'blasphemous' novel *The Satanic Verses* has come to define their level of intolerance, and by extension, Islam as an intolerant religion that doesn't permit dissent or debate.

India was the first non-Muslim country to ban the novel after Syed Shahabuddin, a diplomat-turned-politician who later led the disastrous Babri masjid movement, orchestrated a threatening campaign to stop its distribution. Not content with securing state censorship in the name of Muslim sensitivities, thus depriving others who may have wanted to read the novel, he and his supporters physically attacked and intimidated anyone who dared to speak up for a writer's right to free speech. Historian Mushirul Hasan was beaten up for suggesting that burning and banning of books in the name of religious sensitivities was a bad idea. Salman Khurshid, another politician who has thrived on Muslim 'grievances', sought to justify attacks on Professor Hasan saying that he should be prepared to pay the price for his beliefs.

Forget fundamentalists, even liberal Muslims hedged their bets. Clearly it was not their finest hour.

Twenty-five years later, nothing much appears to have changed with Muslims, still very sensitive to any perceived 'insult' of Islam. Newspaper editors and publishers are having to constantly factor in Muslim sensitivities before publishing anything on Islam. A publisher friend told me how there was a huge debate within his company when they were planning to bring out an Indian edition of Irshad Manji's controversial book, *The Trouble with Islam Today*, a few years ago. The distributors went through it with a toothcomb to satisfy themselves that it did not contain anything that could inflame Muslim passions.

However, things are looking up, and were there to be a Rushdie-like affair today Messrs Shahabuddin and Khurshid may struggle to get support. Young Muslims say they have no time for such 'distractions' from the far more pressing issues that the community needs to address. Any criticism of Islam still arouses strong passions but, in the words of one young woman doctor, 'we don't have to make a spectacle of ourselves every time someone says or writes something provocative'.

Sakeena Qureshi, her head duly covered with a hijab, was firmly against violent or abusive forms of protest.

'We must protest but there are civilized ways of registering your protest, which is to argue it out. Islam teaches tolerance. There is this well-known anecdote about a woman who made it a daily ritual to hurl down garbage from her balcony precisely whenever the Prophet went past her house, but he never protested. One day, there was no woman, no garbage. He wondered what happened to her and knocked at her door to find out if she was all right. The woman apologized to him for her behaviour, and said he had shamed her into realizing her error.'

Muslims like Sakeena Qureshi are no shrinking violets and firmly believe that Muslims have a right to air their resentment in pubic if they believe that their religious sentiments have been hurt. But they draw the line at violence and censorship. Those who whip up violent passions in the name of Islam are 'the worst enemies of Islam', according to them. They also point out that if Muslims want to occupy a moral high ground vis-à-vis Hindu fanatics, such as those who targeted M.F. Husain over his nude paintings of Hindu goddesses ultimately driving him out of the country, then they need to behave differently themselves. A campaign of violence and intimidation by Hindu groups forced India's most famous painter to flee the country in 2006 and seek refuge in Dubai, later acquiring citizenship of Qatar. He never returned to India and died in London in 2011.

'If we are going to resort to violence then what's the difference between us and the Bajrang Dal goons who attacked Husain? What moral right do we have to criticise them?' asked Faraz Alalm, a bank manager.

The idea of banning books is losing its appeal even among many of those who were in the forefront of the campaign for banning *The Satanic Verses*. One must stress that this doesn't mean that every young and 'modern' Muslim is tolerant. There are still many whose level of intolerance would have pleased the anti-Rushdie 'mob'. But, crucially, what has changed is that 'the mob' no longer holds sway. Those who speak the language of the mob are getting increasingly isolated. There are signs of greater openness and, unlike in the past, it is possible nowadays to have a rational discussion at least. Today you can defend other people's right to hold a different opinion without inviting the wrath of the Muslim thought police. It might seem like a small step but, in terms of the Muslim mindset, it is a huge leap forward.

Throughout this book I've tried to emphasise that 'change' and 'progress' in Muslim attitudes must be measured in relative terms—in relation to what they were about ten years ago when the community appeared to be progressively regressing. At last an attempt is being made—slow and patchy though it maybe—to open up closed minds. Ten years from now, you may actually find them reading *The Satanic Verses* without feeling the need to swear at its author.

12
The Muslim Experience

Muslims are often accused of carrying a chip on their shoulders and suffering from self-persecution complex when they grumble about their problems—the pressures and prejudices they face because of their religion. Muslims call it a 'siege mentality' arising from the fact that they feel they are under constant scrutiny.

My non-Muslim friends are often irritated when I tell them that they wouldn't understand what it is like to be a minority group.

'I don't really get this siege mentality business you Muslims go on about,' a non-Muslim friend, a single mother, often tells me. Yet she never tires of complaining about the pressures on her as a lone parent and how a single mother is sought to be 'judged constantly'.

What she doesn't admit is that she suffers from the same 'siege mentality' syndrome that she accuses Muslims of. It is not the Muslims alone who feel paranoid. All minority groups—religious, linguistic, racial, or gender—do. And there's a good reason for it. For they have experiences that are unique to them by virtue of being a minority. The pressures and prejudices that Muslims in India face in their everyday lives are only a version of what a woman in a male-dominated society does; or a single-mother in a two-parent 'conventional' society does; or a gay does in a heterosexual world. And it does not always have to do with discriminatory laws or a deliberate policy to target the minorities. It is in the nature of the beast called 'majority' to take the minorities for granted—and, in extreme cases, not only be insensitive to those 'not like us' but be deliberately cruel to them. They feel a sense of entitlement that comes from being the 'lord of the ring'. The sheer clout that they enjoy because of their numerical strength makes them indifferent to those they see as 'others' or 'outsiders'.

Not surprisingly, the Hindus in India have a similar sense of entitlement (one would have been surprised if they didn't) just as Muslims have in Muslim-majority countries. Still when you're at the wrong end of it, it hurts. So, what's it like for a Muslim to be growing up in India? I put this question to a large cross-section of Muslims, and to be honest, I was a bit surprised by some of the sharp reactions, particularly from the older generation who seemed more sensitive to any perceived slight. The young were more relaxed. They understood that being in a minority is never fun. So better bear it and grin. They were also more keen to emphasise their Indianness, insisting that they saw no conflict between their religious and national identities. They said they felt 'insulted' when asked whether they were 'Muslims first or Indians first'. Such a distinction, they claimed, never even occurred to them.

A common complaint, more widespread among the older generation, is that they are often made to feel as outsiders. India, they say, is still regarded by many Hindus as *their* country alone. There is a tendency to assert the Hindu ownership of India and imply that non-Hindus live at their pleasure. Muslims were particularly hurt when during the campaign to build a Ram temple at the site of Babri Masjid, campaigners insisted that 'this is *our* country and we will do what we like'. The implication, they point out, was that Muslims were not Indians or lesser Indians and, therefore, had no right to protect their place of worship. Referring to Saudi Arabia as 'your Saudi Arabia' or Pakistan as 'your Pakistan' to rub in Muslims' Islamic identity is commonplace.

Older Muslims recall that in the 1960s and the 1970s it was common to be told to 'go to Pakistan if you are not happy here'. Even now, Pakistan is always the ghost in the room. During India-Pakistan cricket matches, I have had well-meaning Hindus come to me and say: 'Huzoor aap ke Pakistani dost bahut accha khel rahen hain' (your Pakistani friends are playing very well).

An Indian Muslim's daily life is marked by reminders of their 'outsider' status. Even well-adjusted younger Muslims—the harbingers of India's 'Muslim spring'—who don't share the paranoia of their elders, say they find it a hard slog at times. To be a Muslim in India means losing innocence at an early age and learning to live with covert suspicion, prejudice and discrimination. It means being reminded every now and then that 'you are not one of us'.

'You learn very early in your life to know your place. As a Muslim you need to develop a very thick skin if you want to retain your sanity,' said a female primary school teacher who only gave her name as 'Ashrafa'.

For many, the demolition of Babri Masjid was a defining moment in their understanding of what it was like to be a Muslim. Not only did it make them conscious of their Muslim identity but, for the first time, they found themselves questioning the nature of Indian secularism and Hindu liberalism.

'Suddenly we came of age,' Mehar Rahman said.

They had barely begun to get over the Ayodhya trauma when 9/11 happened. In its aftermath, every Muslim came to be suspected as a potential terrorist. It was lumped with all previous and subsequent al-Qaeda-inspired attacks in different parts of the world to portray Islam as a 'violent' religion. Violence, it was stated, was inherent in Islam; and jihad was nothing but terrorism by another name.

No amount of Muslim condemnation of terrorism helped and, as Shabana Azmi said in her 2009 London speech, 'When we protested they said, "no, no we're not saying all Muslims are terrorists but it is also a fact that all terrorists are Muslims." What nonsense! Are all Tamil Tigers Muslim? Are all Naxals Muslims? Or are all so-called Maoist guerrillas Muslims? Such sweeping generalisations don't help. It puts the whole community on the defensive. When you are called a Muslim as though it were a term of abuse it makes you edgy...and makes it difficult for you to be objective about your community.'

There are historical parallels to what is happening to Muslims today, and this is not the first time that a whole community or group has been tarred with the same brush because of the sins of some of its members. Think of the demonization of Jews in 1930s' Europe; think of the Nazi label pinned on all Germans because of what the Nazis did to the Jews; think of the Irish at the height of the Troubles; and, nearer home, think of the Sikhs during the Khalistan movement when the entire community came to be labelled as terrorists. Worrying and outrageous though the current wave of Islamophobia is, there is nothing unique about a community being forced to pay the price for the actions of its fanatic fringe.

The more problematic bit for me is the state's role in encouraging such prejudice by using the media and its own law enforcement and intelligence agencies. When the state ceases to be neutral and effectively becomes a party to a veritable witch-hunt on the basis of race, religion or ethnicity, we are in very dangerous territory. And that's what seems to be happening in India. The Indian state is widely seen to be grossly compromised over its treatment of Muslims in the so-called 'war on terror' with its security agencies giving up any pretence of professional objectivity and converting what should have been a fight against terrorism into a fight against Muslims. The result is that today even moderate Muslims feel alienated. More worryingly, it has made the task of moderate Muslims in combating extremism more difficult while, at the same time, making it easier for radical groups to portray themselves as protectors of Islam and the community.

Speak to any Muslim—young or old; men or women; alleged fifth columnists or those willing to 'die' for the country; moderates or extremists; liberals or conservatives—and all you will hear are angry voices. The fury is palpable and has started to undermine their faith in the Indian state's professed secularism. There is also a sense of bewilderment at being portrayed as terrorists. For, it is important to remember, despite their perceived fundamentalism, Indian Muslims have remained largely free from the 'jihadi' contagion—a fact even acknowledged by Islamophobic American diplomats as revealed in their secret cables leaked by the whistleblowing website WikiLeaks in 2011.

It is a pity that instead of building on this advantage and co-opting them as allies in its anti-terrorism efforts, the Indian state has frittered it away in its cynical pursuit of cheap popularity among the Hindu Right. After all there are votes to be had by branding Muslims as terrorists. So, within hours of a terror attack or a foiled plot, police and intelligence agencies start pointing the finger of suspicion at Muslim groups with an obliging media dutifully regurgitating official claims about Muslim involvement. Such claims are never made on record but planted on pliable journalists in background briefings attributed to anonymous sources. Then follows a round-up of Muslims amid breathless media reports about their 'links' with Pakistani terror groups. Never mind if most of them are later found innocent. The intended message—i.e. Muslims were behind yet another terror attack or plot—has gone home. The news that they had been framed either goes unreported or is tucked away where it is guaranteed to go unnoticed. Come the next terror attack, and the drill—the round-ups, the media hype—starts all over again.

The policy is alienating the very Muslim opinion that the government needs on its side if it is serious about winning the hearts and minds of the community. Pro-reform Muslims are worried and regard such tactics extremely unhelpful at a time when they are trying so hard to get the community to come out of its shell. They warn that the new mood of hope and optimism they have been able to generate could very quickly darken if the government is seen to be targeting Muslims to win the Hindu votes.

13
A 'Witch-Hunt'

'Seventy years ago, US soldiers bearing bayoneted rifles came marching up to the front door of our family's home in Los Angeles, ordering us out. Our crime was looking like the people who had bombed Pearl Harbour a few months before. I'll never forget that day, nor the tears streaming down my mother's face as we were forcibly removed, herded off like animals, to a nearby race track. There, for weeks, we would live in a filthy horse stable while our 'permanent' relocation camp was being constructed thousands of miles away in Arkansas, in a place called Rowhwer....

The tragedy of the internment of 120,000 Japanese Americans was not only that it was the greatest violation of our constitutional guarantees, but that it broke apart families and whole communities, and left scars that today remain unhealed, even after the government later apologized and issued reparations.' (My Wartime Internment, George Takei, actor who appeared in the original Star Trek series, *The Guardian*, 27 April 2012).

Substitute Los Angeles with any Indian city—Moradabad, Aligarh, Pune, Delhi, Mumbai, Hyderabad—and this could well have been written by an Indian Muslim harassed by security forces for 'looking like the people' who carry out terror attacks. Ironically, the Indian government protests so vociferously—and rightly—when high-profile Indian Muslims like Shah Rukh

Khan are victims of ethnic profiling at western airports, but has no qualms harassing its own Muslim citizens on similar grounds. This has led to a climate of fear in which Muslims say they don't feel safe.

Abid Shah, who works for an international NGO, says that having seen many of his friends harassed by the police he lives in constant fear.

'If there is a blast in Delhi I make sure that I reach home as soon as possible. There's a sense of siege among Muslims. In my case, it is worse. I am from Kashmir. Being a Muslim is bad enough, but being a Kashmiri makes it a double whammy,' he jokes.

Certain categories of Muslims—the overtly religious types and those with links to a Muslim institution or a Muslim group—feel specially threatened. Most Muslims say they know someone—a neighbour, a friend, a relation, a friend's friend—who has been harassed after a terror incident, for simply being a Muslim. In the previous chapter I have described how there's now an all-too-familiar drill which kicks in after a terror attack, triggering a round-up of Muslims often without the slightest of evidence. This despite the fact that at least two major atrocities—the 2007 Samjhauta Express and the Makkah Masjid blasts—were masterminded by Hindu extremists, the so-called 'saffron terrorists', after being typically first blamed on Muslims.

Shortly before midnight of 18 February 2007, bombs ripped through two crowded carriages of the Delhi-Lahore Samjhauta Express—a special bi-weekly train service meant to facilitate movement of people between India and Pakistan—as it passed Diwana station near Panipat, 80 kilometres from Delhi. At least 68 people, mostly from Pakistan, were killed and dozens injured. The very next day, police and intelligence sources started briefing the media that Indian Muslim extremist groups such as the Student Islamic Movement of India (SIMI), were suspected to have assisted Pakistan-based Lashkar-e-Toiba and Jaish-e-Mohammed in carrying out the atrocity. Police even released sketches of two alleged suspects and several people, including several SIMI office-bearers who were not only arrested but subjected to narcotics tests in order to obtain confessions. A drunk Pakistani national who, the police claimed, was seen throwing one of the suitcases containing bombs from the train, was also questioned.

Yet it was to take the security services more than a year to achieve a breakthrough during which period Muslims remained under suspicion. Amid continued media frenzy, in September 2008, *India Today* carried an 'exclusive' report claiming: 'Narco analysis tests conducted on three key activists of the banned Students Islamic Movement of India (SIMI) have revealed that its activists had helped carry out the Mumbai train bombings of 11 July 2006 and the Samjhauta Express blasts of January 2007. The bombings were carried out with the help of Pakistani nationals who had come from across the border. The tests were carried out in Bangalore on the general secretary Safdar Nagori, his brother Kamruddin Nagori and Amil Parvez in April this year. The "Nagori 13" were arrested from their hideout in Indore by Madhya Pradesh police in March this year. Results of the narco analyst tests exclusively available with *India Today* have revealed, for the first time, SIMI's direct links with not only the Mumbai train bombings which killed over 200 persons but also links with the Samjhauta Express blast of February 2007 which killed 68 persons.'

Similar breathless reports, based on briefings from intelligence sources, appeared in other newspapers and were broadcast by television channels.

Two months later—in November 2008—it was revealed that the attacks were linked to Prasad Shrikant Purohit, an Indian army officer and a member of the Hindu extremist group Abhinav Bharat. Purohit claimed that he had 'infiltrated' Abhinav Bharat and was simply doing his job of collecting intelligence. Meanwhile, the Rajasthan anti-terrorist squad prepared an 800-page charge-sheet in October 2010 according to which the Samjhauta Express was discussed as a potential target for an attack at a meeting of Hindutva bomb makers in February 2006.

To cut the story short, in December 2010 the National Investigation Agency, which had taken over the probe by then, identified Swami Aseemanad, a former RSS activist, as the mastermind behind the blast. He confessed that Hindutva extremists groups engineered the bombing but later claimed that it had been obtained under duress. He was later chargesheeted as one of the main accused in the case along with Sadhvi Pragya Thakur, a self-styled 'godwoman', and is awaiting trial at the time of writing (May 2013). Others arrested for their role in the blast include Kamal Chouhan, another former RSS worker. He is suspected to have planted the bombs with his accomplice Chaudhary, alias Samandar Das.

Aseemanand has also been linked to the Makkah Masjid blasts in Hyderabad on 18 May 2007 in which 14 people were killed, and a series of other terror attacks including those in the Maharashtra towns of Malegaon and Modasa in 2008, and the Ajmer Sharif Darga blast in October 2007 which, again, was initially blamed on Muslim groups.

I have gone at some length to narrate these incidents here not to score points about saffron or green terrorism but to underline how the government agencies and the media have created an atmosphere in which it has become all too easy to pin every act of terrorism on Muslims. In recent years, hundreds of innocent Muslims, young and old, have been thrown into jail on the basis of nothing more than vague suspicion. Many have been held for years without charge. Quite a few have had their careers destroyed in the process.

Take the case of Dr Anwar Ali Javed Ali Khan who spent eight years in jail and whose ordeal still continues. Khan(47) was an Urdu lecturer at the National Defence Academy (NDA), Pune when he was arrested on 11 May 2003, on suspicion of his involvement in a bomb blast in Mulund, Mumbai, in March that year. After languishing for one year in prison he was discharged by a special judge who tried the case under the Prevention of Terrorism Act (POTA) for lack of evidence. But, promptly, he was re-arrested in connection with bomb blasts in the Mumbai suburbs of Mulund and Vile Parle in 2003. He was to spend another eight years behind bars before being granted bail in 2011. But at the time of writing (May 2013) the case is still pending. Meanwhile he lost his job at NDA, and with the tag of a terror suspect attached to him nobody is willing to hire him. Even his former employers have shunned him. While in jail he did a PhD and wrote a book, '*Learn Urdu in 30 days*', which went into three editions. He says he was arrested simply because he was associated with efforts by some friends to set up a legal aid cell—the Muslim Legal Aid and Welfare Foundation—to help Muslims accused of terrorism.

'It was in the initial stages of planning. We wanted a board of patrons and had three meetings. During the initial questioning, the police wanted to know about the meetings. I told them we didn't plan any bomb blast...I wasn't expecting to be arrested and arraigned. It took time for me to adjust and I tried to mentally prepare myself for the ordeal. Jail is a life of deprivation. I missed everything—my family, teaching,' he told *The Hindu* (30 April 2013). Khan sees himself as a victim of a Muslim 'witch-hunt'.

The scale of this 'witch-hunt' has been comprehensively documented in *What it Means to be an Indian Today,* a compilation of testimonies of victims and their families edited by Shabnam Hashmi, a leading social activist and published by ANHAD (Act Now for Harmony and Democracy). The testimonies, taken at two separate people's tribunals held in Hyderabad in 2008 and 2009, make harrowing reading. 'Many a testimonies moistened the eyes of some of the jury members, the harrowing stories of mothers whose sons are being tortured, the wives whose husbands have been made the victim of police atrocities, the third degree torture inside the police custody, the insensitivity of administration was all there, and was registered with the pain and objectivity it deserved...This victimization and demonisation of Muslims in the guise of investigation of terror offences, is having a very serious psychological impact on the minds of not only the families of the victims but also other members of the community. It is leading to a very strong sense of insecurity and alienation which may lead to frightful consequences for the nation,' the report says.

Since then the situation has worsened, pushing it to the top of the list of Muslim concerns. It has become such an emotive issue that, reformists fear, it has the potential of being used by fundamentalist elements to rally their troops and bounce back on the back of the community's growing sense of insecurity. A prominent liberal Muslim journalist said the police tactics in fighting 'Muslim terror' were proving to be a 'god-send' for the 'mullah class' always on the lookout for issues to whip up emotions.

'I can see them salivating…here's an issue waiting to be exploited and they are not going to let go of it. The 'Muslim Spring' that you're talking about could just wither on the back of this,' he said.

Liberal Hindus share the frustration of Muslim reformists.

'I can understand how hard it must be to sell the message of hope and optimism in such a climate. They (reformists) have their work cut out,' a prominent Hindu historian told me.

I see it as part of a bigger story—a continuation by other means of the deep-rooted institutional mistrust of Muslims, the notion of Muslims as fifth columnists. Whereas once they were portrayed as covert 'Pakistani agents' today they are branded as an extension of Pakistan-sponsored terror networks. I grew up in a climate where a Muslim could not afford to say anything positive about Pakistan (not that there was ever very much positive to say about it any way) without attracting attention. Muslims visiting the Pakistan High Commission in New Delhi were tailed and the next day someone would turn up at the door to ask questions. Yet, strangely, it feels that that was a more innocent age. The scruffy CID inspector who landed up at your door was invariably apologetic: 'janaab, apni duty kar rahe hain' ('sir, simply doing my duty.'). These days they're more likely to frog-march you to the police station without so much as a by your leave.

In the heat of the debate on the new climate of fear, the point that is often missed is that there is nothing 'new' about Muslims being treated as a 'threat' to national security. The only difference is that in the pre-terror era they were regarded as closet Pakistani spies (though, in the real world, more non-Muslims have been caught spying for Pakistan than Muslims) while these days they are seen as potential jihadis. The state has become harder and institutional Islamophobia has deepened, as highlighted by the Sachar Committee. It is important to demystify the past: there was never a time when Muslims were trusted by the state security establishment. Latent Islamophobia bubbled just under the surface. All that has happened now is that it has come out in the open. The state has become more brutal in the name of pursuing a police of 'zero tolerance' towards any perceived threat to national security; its biases have become more overt and tactics more crude. Now it is more jackboot than hush-puppies.

Here's a *mea culpa*.

When one is young and idealistic one often deliberately fails to see things and make connections even if they are staring one in the face, because they interfere with one's own idealized vision of the world. In hindsight, those connections look so obvious that you want to kick yourself. I, too, plead guilty on this score. As a young Muslim high on idealism and an unquestioning faith in Indian secularism, I failed to notice the connection between the Congress Party's self-serving brand of secularism and the rise of Muslim fundamentalism—a connection that was to prove dear to Muslims.

Its appeasement of the 'mullahs' and self-styled Muslim 'leaders' in order to garner Muslim votes was mainly responsible for boosting the hold of fundamentalists on the community. Moderate Muslims, feeling marginalized, withdrew from the mainstream leading to widespread alienation. A more damaging consequence of this policy was that it sparked an anti-Muslim backlash and accusations of 'minority appeasement' even though the common Muslim did not benefit from it. Slowly, the resentment began to seep into the government bureaucracy, leading to a covert anti-Muslim state bias which remains deeply embedded even today.

Fundamentalists thrived on growing Muslim alienation, exploiting it to demand concessions on emotive issues such as non-interference in sharia laws and ban on books they did not like. None of these had anything to do with the community's social or economic welfare, and yet, the perception was created that Muslims were being given special treatment. The appeasement of vote-bearing fundamentalists set in motion a vicious circle that saw every concession to the Muslim Right being matched by a concession to the Hindu Right. Books were banned, films were pulled, art shows were stopped, and sporting events were scrapped under a policy of competitive appeasement of minority and majority fundamentalism. National embarrassments such as the Shah Bano case, the Ayodhya debacle, and the Rushdie affair were a direct consequence of what began as a Congress ploy to win Muslim votes.

It is significant that the decline of Muslim fundamentalism has coincided with the decline in the fortunes of the Congress party. Note that the generation of Muslims which is challenging fundamentalism came of age in the era of post-Congress supremacy—after the party had lost its power of patronage and was no longer able to manipulate Muslim sentiments.

Since returning to power in 2004 (at the time of writing, May 2013, there is much speculation whether it would be able to pull it off again at next year's general election), the Congress has tried to tread more cautiously but deeply embedded old habits mean that its Muslim policy is still very much swayed by electoral considerations. It must learn lessons from its past mistakes if it wants to regain the Muslim trust. And that will mean weeding out its old and discredited Muslim cronies who are still hanging around, and throwing its weight behind progressive groups and individuals. More crucially, it must abandon policies/tactics that are guaranteed to play into the hands of fundamentalist elements and derail India's nascent 'Muslim spring'. Using the state security apparatus to terrorize Muslims in the name of fighting terror is one such policy. It is a ticking bomb that needs to be defused, pronto.

For the first time since independence, Muslims are trying to get a new life and there is a real prospect of a more-integrated and forward looking Muslim community emerging from the churning it is undergoing. I dislike hyperbole but it is a historic moment in the life of Indian Muslims and it will be a real shame if it is allowed to be lost because of the state's misguided policies or lack of support from the wider civil society.

14
The Pakistan Connection

Lucky is the Muslim who, sometime or the other, has not been made to feel—through winks and nudges—like a closet Pakistani with 'divided loyalties'. Among other things, being a Muslim in India means having to constantly wrestle with the so-called 'Pakistani connection'. It means to be always conscious that one is being watched for pro-Pakistani views. Pakistan is apparently every Indian Muslim's alleged dirty secret. *The* skeleton in the cupboard.

I have heard it said that 'scratch a Muslim and you will find a Pakistani heart beating'. Lines such as 'your Pakistan' or 'your Pakistani friends' (even 'your countrymen') are thrown almost casually at Muslims. Often the speaker is not even conscious of the import of what he or she said.

Once I protested to a friend after he had said something along those lines. He said I was 'over-reacting'. For a moment I thought maybe I was, and felt slightly ridiculous, but then it occurred to me: would he have said 'your Pakistan' to a non-Muslim? A Muslim cannot say anything remotely complimentary about Pakistan, such as praise a Pakistani cricketer or a writer, without raising eyebrows.

'You're saying this because she is a Pakistani,' one friend told me when I said that Kamila Shamsie was a better novelist than a certain young Indian writer we were discussing. This from a person who has more Pakistani friends than me, and whose multicultural credentials are impeccable.

The most testing time for Indian Muslims is when India and Pakistan play each other in a sporting event, especially cricket, and more particularly if it is on Indian soil. Thanks to the behaviour of a tiny minority of Muslims who notoriously root for Pakistan, it is assumed that every Muslim does. We hear rumours, invariably baseless, of how Muslims offer special prayers in mosques for Pakistan to win.

The most common character in Hindi cinema is a Muslim army or police officer who is caught selling Indian intelligence secrets to Pakistan. Even someone as overtly 'nationalist' as Shah Rukh Khan, who is married to a Hindu and seldom misses a chance to swear his loyalty to India (a sign of the pressure on Muslims, especially those who are in public life, constantly to prove their Indian-ness), has not been spared. In 2010, there was a furore when he regretted that no Pakistani cricketers were picked to play in an upcoming Indian Premier League (IPL) tournament. The context for his comments was widespread speculation that there had been pressure on owners of IPL teams not to bid for Pakistani cricketers. Shiv Sena and other right-wing Hindu groups threatened to disrupt the screening of his film, *My Name is Khan*, which was due for release. Several cinema houses in Mumbai were attacked and posters of the film were torn. Despite police assurance of protection, a number of cinema chains stopped advance booking for the film.

Sena chief Bal Thackeray called Khan a 'traitor' and a party spokesman, Sanjay Raut, said: 'This is not Shah Rukh, but the Khan in him that's saying all this. Let Shah Rukh go and stay in Lahore, Karachi or Islamabad. He is not needed in Mumbai. (Shiv Sena chief) Balasaheb has made it clear that Pakistani players wouldn't be allowed to play in the IPL or set foot in Maharashtra.'

Initially the actor stood his ground saying he had said nothing that warranted an apology.

'I have done nothing wrong in saying what I said about Pakistani players, and I said that as an Indian,' he said.

But faced with threats to his film, he was forced to sue for peace and issue a statement clarifying that his remarks about Pakistani cricketers had been 'misunderstood'.

Tennis player Sania Mirza had her patriotism questioned when she decided to marry Pakistani cricketer Shoib Malik. Bal Thackeray said that 'had Sania's heart been Indian, it wouldn't have beaten for a Pakistani. Henceforth, Sania will not remain an Indian. If she wished to play for India, she should have chosen an Indian life partner,' he wrote in an editorial in his party's mouthpiece *Saamana*.

Yet no eyebrows were raised when Bollywood star of yesteryears Reena Roy married another Pakistani cricketer Mohsin Khan in 1983.

Muslims' own attitude towards Pakistan is mostly of a vague sense of affinity through family ties as most Indian Muslims have some family link in Pakistan, however remote—long-lost uncles, cousins, aunts, nephews and nieces. They tend to become defensive when branded as closet pro-Pakistanis. But contrary to propaganda, the fact is that they have no emotional attachment to Pakistan except, perhaps, for a fringe element. The media coverage given to pro-Pakistani Muslims is grossly disproportionate to their number.

The younger generation of Indian Muslims has a less complicated relationship with Pakistan. As the old generation on both sides of the border fades, family ties have loosened and become more distant. It is no longer about separated parents, siblings, uncles and nephews. The young, both in India and Pakistan, are now several generations removed from their relations across the 'other side'. Some have never met their Pakistani relations.

Take my own case, and I am not young. My Pakistani connection was through my parents and their relations in Pakistan: they wrote to each other, and my Pakistani uncle and his family visited India occasionally. But with both my parents and uncle and aunt now dead, I have no link with Pakistan. I have two nephews there who I last saw in the 1960s. If I were to see them today I would not be able to recognise them. I have never met their families or know anything about them.

Mine is not an atypical case. It is true of every Muslim family. Today's Muslims simply don't feel the same way about Pakistan that their ancestors did because of their family links—and their concern for people from whom they had been so recently separated. Free from the emotional baggage of their parents, young Muslims, like any other Indian, have only an academic interest in Pakistan. Given the widespread misconception about Muslim attitudes towards Pakistan, it is important to emphasise that, contrary to conventional wisdom, their so-called 'soft corner' for it was never about religion or pan-Islamic solidarity. It was always about family ties, and as those ties have loosened—almost dissolved in most cases—Pakistan has become just another country for them.

But there is another, more fundamental, factor that separates Indian Muslims from their Pakistani counterparts—indeed from Muslims of all theocratic Islamic states despite the growing influence of Saudi Arabia's strident Islam globally. There is a joke about three Muslims—an Indian, a Pakistani, and a Bangladeshi—who were walking through a subway in London when they saw a white teenager mug an elderly woman and run away with her handbag. The Pakistani said, 'Too much bloody lawlessness...this sort of thing wouldn't happen in Saudi Arabia.'

The Bangladeshi, nodding his head in agreement, said: 'Yes, there he would have his hands chopped...and right too.'

The Indian said: 'Guys, come on let's help the woman and call the police.' Obviously the joke has been invented by Indian Muslims to make fun of *sharia*-obsessed Pakistani and Bangladeshis, but it is not completely off the wall. I will not rule out such a scenario playing out in real life. For the fact is that Indian Muslims *are* different from their Pakistani and Bangladeshi peers. A British Council survey in April 2013 revealed that more Pakistani youth would prefer to live under Islamic law than democracy.

'When asked to pick the best political system, both sharia and military rule were favoured over democracy,' the survey said.

In Bangladesh, Islamist groups operating under the banner of Hefajat, are engaged in a violent street campaign for the introduction of sharia and anti-blasphemy laws; gender segregation with a ban on men and women mixing in public; a crackdown on 'shameless behaviour and dresses'; and the reformist Ahmadiyya sect to be declared non-Muslim. In Pakistan, Ahmadiyyas are already regarded as non-Muslims and denied full democratic rights.

All this is in sharp contrast to the Muslim attitudes in India. Indian Muslims have happily co-existed with Ahmadiyyas even though they may not approve of some of their practices and beliefs, especially the claim of their founder Mirza Ghulam Ahmad to be a prophet. In fact, it was in India that the sect was founded in 1889 and it never faced any persecution.

It is important to underline that *sharia* has never been on the agenda of Indian Muslims. Even on the issue of Muslim Personal Law they are deeply divided, especially after the Shah Bano case when an old and destitute divorcee (see *The Shah Bano effect*) was denied maintenance by her husband. Indian Muslims cherish the freedoms they enjoy by virtue of being citizens of a democratic and secular country and have no appetite for authoritarianism even if it is dressed up in Islamic colours. Indian Muslims who live in Islamic countries never tire of complaining how oppressed they feel despite being among the believers. True, there is a creeping influence of Arab Islam, notably Saudi's Wahhabi brand, manifested in the clamour for visible Islamic symbols like beard and hijab, but Indian Islam is too eclectic to be shackled by any one rigid tendency. The roots of Sufi traditions of Indian Islam are too deep to be trifled with easily. (Even in Kashmir, foreign militants have not been able to impose their brand of Islam). A visit to a Sufi shrine such as Ajmer Sharif and Nizamuddin Aulia, thronged by thousands of devotees at any given time, is enough to convince you that Indian Islam is well and alive. Indian Islam is the product of centuries of mingling of what is called 'ganga-jamuni tehzeeb'—a confluence of Hindu-Muslim cultural traditions.

Indian Muslims are more influenced by Islamic culture (a fusion of Persian and Mughal cultures later influenced by Hindu cultural traditions of northern India) than its fundamentalist religious aspects as found in the more stark Arab strand of Islam. Pakistani Muslims used to be like us until the country's 'Islamization' under President Zia-ul-Haq. During his ten-year rule (1978-1988), Pakistan was turned into a mini-Saudi Arabia with the introduction of a harsh sharia regime and anti-blasphemy law. Indian Muslims never reconciled to the 'new' Pakistan.

Another factor that has played a role in Indian Muslims distancing themselves from Pakistan is its political and economic collapse, and its descent into terrorism at the same time that India has grown in stature. Many Muslims openly admit that they feel embarrassed at being linked to Pakistan. Not wanting to be associated with a failed state is part of a wider Indian trend. In Britain, Indian expatriates who are mostly better educated and economically more prosperous than their Pakistani and Bangladeshi peers, insist on being referred to as 'British Indians' rather than 'British Asians'—the official generic term for immigrants from the subcontinent—to avoid being confused with their poorer cousins from Lahore and Dhaka.

Never before since its creation have Indian Muslims been more detached from Pakistan than they are today. Yet, they continue to be targets of a campaign designed to question their Indian loyalties by casting them as pro-Pakistani. It fits in with the Hindu Right's wider hate agenda and helps it keep the bogey of a 'Muslim threat' alive. The challenge for Muslims is not to be provoked. They need to learn to stop being defensive about Pakistan. They have nothing to explain to anyone if their own convictions are right. As Shah Rukh Khan argued, he did not need a certificate of patriotism from others. His father fought for India's independence and he was 'proud' of being the son of an Indian freedom fighter.

Muhammad Ali, the great American boxer, fighting racism told his critics: 'I am America. I am the part you won't recognize. But get used to me. Black, confident, cocky.'

That's the sort of spirit Indian Muslims need today: 'I am India. I am the part you won't recognize. But get used to me...'

It might take them a bit to get used to the 'new' Muslim, but ultimately they will.

15
Victimhood Syndrome

Renowned Urdu poet Akbar Allahabadi was famously prone to exaggeration, and his reasoning was that sometime it was necessary to embellish a dull story to make it interesting (*Badha bhi dete hain kuch zeb-e-dastaan ke liye*).

He could well have been talking about the story of Indian Muslims which has been 'embellished' to a point that it is often hard to recognise it. The image of Muslims as an oppressed group barely able to breathe under the weight of Hindu jackboot has always struck me as a gross exaggeration. A crude caricature of a community that is fearlessly vocal, even if most of the time it wastes its vocal chords on highlighting the wrong issues; stands up for its rights though seldom for the right ones; and which, despite its 'plight', is happier living in a free and democratic country than an Islamic republic.

Ask any Indian Muslim of any hue (except Kashmiri Muslims, but that's another story altogether) whether, given a chance, they would opt to leave India, and the answer is a loud 'no'. Indeed, quite a few Muslims who moved to Pakistan after partition were to return soon—disillusioned and a little ashamed. One line I heard repeatedly during my research for this book was that India is 'the best place for Muslims' and they wouldn't exchange it for any other country.

So, how did this perception of 'oppressed' Muslims waiting

for the next flight out of India come about? It started with the Muslims who went over to Pakistan—the so-called 'mohajirs' keen to justify their decision to migrate. They did this by advertising their new homeland as a land of opportunities, where Muslims were the masters of their own destiny and could walk tall, and 'contrasting' it with the 'plight' of the 'bechare' (hapless) Indian Muslims 'oppressed' and discriminated against by vindictive Hindus. They insisted on referring to India as 'Bharat' to signify its 'Hindu' character, and described it as 'dozakh' (hell) where Muslims were condemned to die a slow death. Pakistan, of course, was a 'holy land'.

Pakistanis routinely taunted Indian Muslims for staying on in a country where, they were told, they had no future. I remember my uncle—a big cheese in Pakistan's newly-minted corporate sector—telling my father what a 'big mistake' he had made by deciding to stay on in India.

'There's nothing here for Muslims. Come to Pakistan. We'll make sure you've a great future,' he would say while my cousins turned up their noses at the sight of the lowly Ambassador car and rickety Delhi transport buses, contrasting them with imported limousines they had back in Pakistan.

It may have ended there. But then India shot itself in the foot. A wave of communal (read, anti-Muslim) riots in the 1960, 1970s and 1980s; widespread complaints of discrimination in jobs and housing; and increasingly shrill anti-Muslim rhetoric of the RSS and its outfits not only played into the Pakistani propaganda but created a wider perception, especially in the Muslim world, that India was not treating its Muslims fairly and in a manner consistent with its constitutional guarantees. The forcible demolition of Babri Masjid in 1992, in an unprecedented display of Hindu majoritarian might, and the massacre of Muslims in Gujarat in 2002 reinforced that perception.

Slowly, sections of Muslims too started to see themselves as 'victims'. The idea of 'victimhood' suited those who, for lack of education and/or skills, were simply unemployable but could use conspiracy theories to cover up their own incompetence. They shouted the loudest about anti-Muslim discrimination. Over time, there developed a vested interest among sections of Muslims to portray themselves as a persecuted people.

No doubt that there have been moments when Muslims have been under great pressure. The BJP's Ayodhya campaign was one such occasion. But that does not qualify for Muslims to be defined as an oppressed and persecuted minority. A religious minority is 'persecuted' when its right to exercise its religious beliefs is restricted. Indian Muslims face no such restrictions. The country is full of mosques; major Muslim festivals are marked by national holidays; the state actively facilitates public celebration or observance of Muslim practices, often at considerable inconvenience to the public with roads closed for hours, for example, during Muharram processions or on Eid.

Persecuted minorities don't enjoy constitutional protection as Indian Muslims do. Ask the Bohras in Pakistan; Bahai's in Iran; or Arabs living in Israel and they will tell you what it means to be a persecuted minority. In fact, Indian Muslims are perhaps among the most well-protected religious minority groups anywhere in the world. Muslims even in many Islamic countries (the shias in Sunni Saudi Arabia and the sunnis in Shia Iran) don't enjoy the same level of state protection as Indian Muslims do in 'Hindu India'.

So the image of the 'bechara mussalman' that has come to define India's Muslim community is a typical case of embellishing a tale to make it more engaging. But this does not mean, as I have shown in previous chapters, that it is all hunky-dory. The truth is that Muslims are not treated fairly and over the years anti-Muslim bias has become institutionalised, with the security establishment particularly hostile to Muslims. Inevitably, this has caused alienation and created a siege mentality that does not help reform. Muslims need to be assured that the state is on their side and not against them. This will require a change in the mindset at the highest level, starting with the political class and top bureaucracy, which has been a major source of grief for Muslims. Muslims don't want special treatment. What they want is to be treated as normal Indian citizens, not punished for being Muslims.

16
The Enemy Within

One of the biggest misfortunes of Indian Muslims has been their leadership. Cynical, opportunistic and woefully unrepresentative of the community, it has done more damage to Muslim interests than the perceived enemies. It's the enemy within—and the more dangerous for it. Six decades of incompetent and corrupt leadership has driven Muslims into a blind alley. A dead end piled high with problems caused by a self-serving agenda of personal advancement and cronyism.

It is a direct consequence of the wrong priorities pursued by successive generations of mostly self-styled leaders that, so many decades after independence, Muslims are begging to be recognised as an economically and socially backward class so that they get can reservations in jobs. Ordinary poor Muslims struggling to make two ends meet were told by their leaders that protecting religious identity and saving neglected mosques was a greater priority than getting them out of the vicious circle of poverty and illiteracy.

It is not an accident of history, as is often sought to be made out, that Indian Muslims lead parallel lives stuck on a planet altogether different from that inhabited by their non-Muslim fellow Indians. This is how it was arranged by Muslim leaders and their political, mostly Congress, patrons. They had a deal whereby feudal landlords and later, their sons and daughters, with power to deliver Muslim votes were recognised as community leaders and rewarded with seats in parliament, and plum posts in the government. For this deal to work it was important for the community to be kept backward and dependant on their leaders' patronage, which they could then cash into votes at election time.

While masquerading as protectors of their community, Muslim leaders have actively conspired to keep it weak in order to exploit its vulnerability. Muslim leadership has become a lucrative dynastic business with the baton passing from one generation to another.

In the Old Delhi neighbourhood, where I spent my childhood, the local Muslim leadership comprised semi-educated and conservative mullahs with links to the Congress or Jamaat-e-Islami. They had no interest in the welfare of the people they claimed to 'lead', and denounced anyone who talked about change. My parents were branded 'atheists' and hounded. My mother, an activist of the Communist Party of India's women's wing, was denounced as a 'Russian agent' and accused of 'brainwashing' Muslim women because she led a campaign to educate them and raise their social awareness.

This type of Muslim leadership was replicated across the country. Little has changed over the past half century. There has never been any grassroots Muslim activism except in the form of moral policing. Muslims must be the only community without any credible organisation engaged in reform.

The current change in the community is being driven by individuals in what looks like the start of a belated backlash against institutional leadership. Rebellion is brewing even in conservative Muslim ghettoes whose denizens were once regarded as dumb cattle who could be herded any which way on the back of emotive slogans. It seems like only yesterday when the Shahi Imam of Delhi's Jama Masjid could sway Muslim voters across the country simply with a fiery Friday sermon. Political leaders queued up to humour him. Now even people living on the steps of Jama Masjid don't bother about him. They mockingly refer to the current Imam, Syed Ahmed Bukhari, son of the late Syed Abdullah Bukhari, as a clown. (His father was a famous political power broker but even his influence started to decline while he was still alive.) You hear variations of this epithet wherever you go—and in relation to all variety of Muslim leaders.

The fragmentation of the Muslim vote (the 2012 state elections in Uttar Pradesh saw the Muslim vote divided three-ways between the Samajwadi Party, the Bahujan Samaj Party and the Congress) is the clearest illustration of how the old leadership is losing its grip, with more and more Muslims making independent choices—voting for candidates and parties who, they believe, will address their real day-to-day concerns. And, if they don't deliver they get a kicking in the next election. No party or a candidate can now expect to have a permanent lease on the Muslim vote. There is no such thing as a 'Muslim vote bank' any more.

At last Muslims have started to determine for themselves what their interests are and who is best placed to address them, rather than being dictated by unrepresentative community leaders. The era of received wisdom is gone. What is particularly significant is a profound change in the Muslim perception of their interests. Increasingly, they are now inclined to see them through the prism of their practical every-day needs—jobs, education, housing—instead of getting excited (as they used to) by emotional cries (a bogey at the best of times) of 'Islam in danger' and 'threat' to Muslim identity'. It is no longer enough to dress up any old thing as a 'Muslim issue' and hope to cash in on it. Whereas once they could be persuaded to jump into the well in the name of religion, today Muslims will not buy anything unless it has a bearing on their social and economic welfare. In a 2006 survey by Delhi-based Centre for the Study of Developing Societies, 69 per cent Muslims identified poverty and unemployment as the most important issues facing the community.

There is an irony in religious issues losing their seductive charm at a time when Indian Muslims, like Muslims around the world, have become more religious in reaction to the post-9/11 Islam-baiting. The past decade has seen an exponential increase in the number of practicing Muslims in India. It is hard to quantify this sort of thing, but you can tell it from the crowds at mosques and the popularity of Ramadan and hajj even among young Muslims. The beards and hijabs tell their own story. Never before in independent India have I heard so many Muslims claim that they offer namaz regularly and observe rozas. The overwhelming majority of 'new mullahs' are young people—the very segment that is trying to move the community away from its obsession with emotive religious issues on to a more secular plane. They have exposed the fallacy that you cannot be religious and modern at the same time; that religiosity is incompatible with a quest for progress.

The old leadership overlooked the fact that like everybody else Muslims have multiple identities. They have their religious identity but they are also citizens of a secular country, and these two identities are not mutually exclusive. Instead, the old leadership focused only on their Muslim identity. Muslims thus came to assume a one-dimensional religious identity seeking solutions to their problems as Muslims rather than as Indian citizens. The new generation is trying to get away from that distorted notion of Muslim identity.

Until now, the Muslim leadership was marked by a complete absence of credible secular figures from the wider Muslim civil society. Muslim academics, businessmen, sports people, showbiz celebrities showed no interest in getting involved in the community's affairs beyond paying lip service. While it is true that politicians and mullahs hijacked the community, what is often overlooked is that this 'hijacking' was made easier by the fact that the secular Muslim elite avoided getting their hands dirty. This left the field free for sectarian clerics and their political mentors to make hay.

Meanwhile, over the years, the so-called 'Muslim debate' has polarized around two extreme viewpoints—the fundamentalists at one end of the extreme and left-wing progressives on the other, both talking 'at' each other rather than to the broader community. In the process, the centrist viewpoint, which is what the majority of Muslims hold, has been lost. It is important to point out that despite the constant lament over a lack of moderate Muslim viewpoint—a perception no doubt inspired partly by the community's own actions—the fact is that the majority of Muslims, like most of their fellow Indians, are located at the centre ground. But because of their partly real, partly imagined insecurities and a felt need to be 'led', they have allowed themselves to be manipulated by a bankrupt leadership. Gradually though this silent majority of moderates has started to find its voice, but for it to be heard it is important that it is given space in the media and, more importantly, a political platform. Political parties must seek out moderate young Muslims and groom them in leadership roles. If the political class and the media do their bit, Indian Muslims can look forward, finally, to be led by people who can take them in the right direction. Just as it is true of a nation, so it is of a community, that it is only as good as its leadership.

Even as I am optimistic about the future of Indian Muslims, history cautions us against jumping the gun too soon. The most promising of revolutionary movements have fizzled out while our 'Muslim spring' has not even taken the form of an organised movement yet. The only thing that can be said with certainty at this stage is that things cannot get worse than they have been so far. When you start from such a low base, they can only get better.

17
Needed: New Ways of Seeing

So, what next? Where do we go from here?

The hardest bit was to get the Muslim community to wake up from its comatose slumber. Now that it has, and is trying to move into a new direction, the first thing that its well-meaning critics must do—as outlined in the previous chapter—is to recognise the effort. This will require a new way of looking at Muslims, and old perceptions will have to go. Much of that perception has its origins in extreme anti-Muslim prejudice rooted in the history of Hindu-Muslim relations. Outsiders may find it hard to grasp the depth of Muslim angst. They say that they feel they have been stripped of their dignity through constant attacks on their loyalty and relentless pressure to prove their 'Indian-ness'. They find it humiliating to be constantly asked whether they are 'Indians first or Muslims first'.

For starters, they need to be given back their dignity and self-respect by treating them as equal citizens. It is time to stop being patronising towards Muslims as though one is dealing with a slightly dim and difficult child who needs a spanking every day. Even if they are difficult at times and lag behind the rest of the class, the modern civilized approach favours empathy—not exclusion.

The media will have to make a conscious effort to highlight moderate Muslim voices instead of continuing to flog the usual suspects. As a journalist who has ridden the beast, I know its nature. There is always pressure on reporters to produce 'interesting' copy, which is not what moderate voices might always yield. Akbar Allahabadi, the popular 20th century Urdu poet who confessed to 'embellishing' his tales to seduce the audience, would have had some sympathy for them.

But the problem with Indian media's coverage of Muslims is not so much of embellishing the tale as of a complete lack of balance. It is much too one-sided and has allowed the fundamentalists/extremists to hijack the Muslim agenda. The claim that moderate Muslims are hard to find or—more bizarrely—that there is no such thing as a moderate Muslim, has worn thin over the years. Moderate Muslims may be less aggressive in pushing their viewpoint than the extremists (and that is true of moderates in all communities and all over the world), but this doesn't mean that other viewpoints don't exist. The problem is that sufficient effort is not made to seek out alternative voices because they don't make 'sexy' copy.

Arguably, there was a time—until the 1980s—when it was not easy to find articulate moderate mainstream Muslims. Today there is no dearth of such voices, but they struggle to be heard, which reinforces the impression of an anti-Muslim bias. A common complaint is that letters or statements issued by moderate Muslims are ignored by newspapers whereas anything inflammatory is guaranteed front page. On television, debates are monopolized by rabble-rousers. If the alternative viewpoint is represented at all, it is by voices regarded by most Muslims as the 'other extreme'—i.e. progressive left-wing Muslims with a reputation for being out of touch with the community. The mainstream middle-of-the-road Muslim viewpoint rarely finds an outlet.

'What about Muslims like me, him or her?' asked an animated Delhi professional pointing to a group of his friends, all practicing Muslims, some sporting beards and wearing hijab.

'We don't fit in either of the two categories: we are not fanatics and we are not revolutionaries. We are normal Muslims who believe in Islam and follow its teachings and rituals. But we are as broad-minded, moderate and secular as any other Indian citizen. But do you ever see us on TV or read about us in newspapers. I have stopped reading newspapers because they are so negative.'

Overtly partisan journalism is one thing: you know where it is coming from, and what to expect. What is not acceptable is journalism which hides its biases behind a façade of objectivity. Using the old tactic of *suppressio veri, suggestio falsi*, large sections of the supposedly objective Indian press have constructed a narrative around Indian Muslims that bears no resemblance to facts. Media reporting plays a big part in creating public perceptions which, in turn, breed prejudices or feed into existing ones. Muslims alone are not victims of such reporting, and it is not special pleading to ask for the media to take a fresh look at the way it reports minority faith and linguistic groups. I have never bought into the notion of journalism as a 'mission'. Journalists are not missionaries. Their job is to inform and they should stick to it without allowing their own biases or other extraneous factors to come in the way of facts.

Another group that needs to rethink its approach is the liberal Muslim intelligentsia which has remained mostly a passive spectator to the developments in the Muslim community, leaving regressive forces to shape the agenda. It won't be fair to blame the liberal Muslims entirely though, for the fact is that they have been effectively shut out of the debate. Because of their often elitist background and patronising stance, they are seen as outsiders with no roots in the community and little understanding of its problems. Their tendency to flaunt their irreligiosity, confusing secularism with atheism, has not helped their cause. Rather than reaching out to ordinary Muslims they have ended up alienating them by constantly talking down to them and taking an uncompromisingly hard line on most issues. Like others they make the mistake of lumping all Muslims together as a homogenous monolith. But, of course, they should know better considering that they themselves are a living refutation of that assumption. If they can be Muslims and yet different from other fellow-Muslims, other Muslims can also be different from each other.

Post-Ayodhya and 9/11, a wave of Islamophobia has made liberal Muslims sit up, and there are signs of a slight shift from the hitherto hands-off approach. But we are still nowhere near the nature and level of liberal engagement needed to make a difference. They must start with trying to win the confidence of the wider community by rethinking their deeply-ingrained antipathy (a hangover from the Soviet Union brand of secularism) to religion. The notion that 'faith equals fundamentalism' or atheism is a precondition for secularism has no basis. And there is no better proof of that than the young practicing Muslims fighting fundamentalism.

But, of course, it takes two to tango. Conservative Muslims, on their part, must stop seeing all liberals as raving Commie atheists on a mission to wipe religion from the face of the earth. Years of mutual mistrust and suspicion must give way in the larger interest of the community if it doesn't want to spend the next 60 years, as it has spent the past 60, in self-imposed darkness, and prey to fanaticism and vote bank politics.

Muslim Institutions

The state of a community's institutions is a good guide to the state of the community itself. Strong and progressive communities are institution-builders and use their institutions for the good and advancement of their members. Weak and regressive communities end up with weak and regressive institutions exploited by sectional interests for their own ends.

Post-independence, Indian Muslims have an appalling record of institution-building. With the odd exception, they have not only *not* built any institution that the community can be proud of but have been busy wrecking those they inherited from a previous generation of great Muslim reformers. Ask anyone to name five decent Muslim institutions built since independence and you will be met with blank stares and an embarrassing silence. Many of the old ones, especially in north India, are in a mess—casualties of wilful neglect and politicization. The biggest casualty has been Aligarh Muslim University, established by the great social reformer Sir Syed Ahmed Khan, in 1875, to provide modern education to Muslims. This once-grand institution, which produced some of the country's finest academics and public figures, has been hijacked by an opportunistic alliance of religious and political interests, and reduced to a glorified ghetto. Constant political interference and crude attempts to hound liberal faculty members such as Irfan Habib, one of India's most respected historians, damaged its reputation to a degree that at one point even Muslim employers didn't want to have anything to do with its graduates. Things have been quieter lately but a covert struggle for control among competing groups is always bubbling under the surface. It's like a ticking bomb that could go off anytime. I am not sure if AMU will be the first choice of even many bright Muslim, let alone non-Muslim, scholars. Which is a pity because it still has some excellent teachers but they are not able to work to their full potential because of an insular academic culture.

Jamia Millia, after years of neglect as a private fiefdom of a small coterie of politicians, has made huge progress since it was taken over by the Government in 1988 and given the status of a central university. Since then it has had two progressive spells: one under late Anwar Jamal Kidwai, the first vice-chancellor after Jamia became a central university; and the other under Mushirul Hasan, the noted historian. Lately there have been signs of old tendencies trying to stage a comeback, and at the time of writing (November 2013), the university is in turmoil again under an interim management, pending the appointment of a new vice chancellor to succeed Najeeb Jung.

Darul Uloom, India's oldest centre of Islamic teaching at Deoband, has been recaptured by the old obscurantist clique after forcing out Ghulam Mohammad Vastanvi, a progressive educationist from Gujarat, barely months after being appointed its vice-chancellor in 2011 (see 'Phoney Fundamentalism'). The murky manoeuvres deployed to unseat him sums up the story of the decline of India's Muslim institutions. And that's the biggest challenge facing Muslim modernizers: saving these cherished institutions from their cannibalizing guardians. It will not be easy. For, although it is a small coterie, it is also very powerful, with its tentacles spread right through the political establishment in Delhi. It will need a long and sustained campaign—not directed against any individual or group but focused on rekindling among Muslims a pride in their institutions. The idea that the ordinary Muslim is indifferent is a bogus one. There was anger on the streets of Deoband when

Vastanvi was thrown out, with ordinary people denouncing it as 'theological terror', and I've seen anger at AMU and in Jamia against fundamentalists. People are looking for the right leadership. The new generation of reform-minded Muslims should seize the moment. It could be a hard slog but it is a fight worth taking on.

Throughout this book I have argued that successive post-independence generations of Indian Muslims bear a huge responsibility—direct or indirect, through acts of commission or omission—for the present state of the community; and a shadow of collective shame and embarrassment hangs over all of us Muslims. It used to be the case that some of us—urban, educated and liberal types—believed that we had the luxury of staying above the fray and watch from our ivory towers as the rest of the wretched community—steeped in backwardness and illiteracy—reeled from the double whammy of its own resident fundamentalists and the Hindu Right. Until, on 6 December 1992, the penny dropped and we realized the impossibility of being half-pregnant—it suddenly dawned on us that we could not call ourselves Muslims, no matter how nominal, and expect to remain immune to what was happening to the rest of the community.

Fence-sitting is no longer a luxury for a Muslim. Everyone will need to muck in and soil their hands if they want the community to be rid of the fundamentalist litter. As the old typing drill went: 'Now is the time for all good men (and women) to come to the aid of the party.'

We are already sixty-six years too late.

18
The Way Forward

Hollywood actor Michael Douglas, recovering from cancer, was interviewed on an American television channel. Douglas said the prognosis was good and doctors were optimistic of a full recovery but he needed a lot of moral and medical support. At the end, the interviewer asked: 'Can I do anything for you?'

Douglas said: 'Give me a hug'.

The analogy might appear slightly stretched but the Indian Muslim community, recovering from a long comatose state, will need more than a hug from friends and well-wishers, notably, the government, to prevent a relapse. It will need concrete help (strong antibiotics and lots of health supplements!) in the shape of government policies, to overcome its deep social and economic backwardness, which has been one of the factors behind the rise of Muslim fundamentalism. Equally important is the need to help restore the community's faith in state machinery which, as I have shown in previous chapters, is at its lowest because of the perception that there is an institutional anti-Muslim bias across government agencies, especially in the security services.

As it happens, the government already has an excellent blueprint before it in the form of the Sachar Committee report. Although it was embraced with remarkable alacrity, seven years have passed and there has been little progress towards implementing it. There are fears that, for all the rhetoric, it seems condemned to go the way of previous such reports—some going back to the days of Jawaharlal Nehru and Indira Gandhi—and end up on the scrapheap. There has also been little headway in pushing through a 15-point programme for minorities, announced by the Manmohan Singh Government in 2006. Among other things, it provided for improved minority access to school education; greater resources for teaching Urdu and modernizing 'madrassas'; and scholarships for meritorious minority students. But the government lost enthusiasm after the BJP objected to allocating government funds for the benefit of religious minorities, calling it 'communal funding' and 'minority appeasement'.

What the government fails to realize is that it is missing a huge opportunity to reconnect with Muslims by dragging its feet on such initiatives. Even if only a few of the Sachar Committee's headline recommendations had been quickly and effectively implemented it would have sent out a positive message to the Muslim community that it was serious about addressing their problems. Still, it is not too late. Arguably, some of the recommendations that require setting up complicated institutional mechanisms will take time but there are many that can be implemented straightway.

A start can be made with a UK-style anti-discrimination law suggested by the Sachar panel, to ban discrimination on the basis of religion, race, gender, sexual orientation or disability. It has also recommended the setting up of an Equal Opportunities Commission on the lines of Britain's Equality and Human Rights Commission, which has powers to enforce the country's anti-discrimination laws.

'While providing a redressal mechanism for different types of discrimination, this will give a further re-assurance to the minorities that any unfair action against them will invite the vigilance of the law,' the committee says.

While about it, the government can emulate another British practice by requiring all its departments and agencies, especially the police, to show that the makeup of their workforce reflects the multicultural and multi-religious diversity of the country. It can be gradually extended to the private sector. In Britain, private companies risk losing government contracts if they are found not to be making a visible effort to recruit people from ethnic groups.

Such steps, already overdue, must be taken quickly in order to dispel Muslim doubts about the impartiality of government machinery, and to restore the community's faith in the secular professions of the Indian state.

Other issues that need immediate attention include equal Muslim access to education, particularly higher education, even if it requires some sort of affirmative action short of a Muslim quota; help with soft bank loans not only for business start- ups but also to fund higher studies and invest in modern housing as an incentive for Muslims to move out of sink estates and ghettos; a pro-active policy to increase Muslim representation in government services; and a targeted campaign to boost literacy, promote birth control, and reduce high infant mortality.

The important thing is to give the community a sense of belonging by treating them as normal citizens. Once a credible mechanism to prevent anti-Muslim discrimination is in place, many of the other factors that are holding Muslims back will take care of themselves, as we have seen in Britain where ethnic minorities are now far better placed than they were before the equal opportunities laws were brought. It is not just enough to bring in laws but to enforce them strictly, though sometime their sheer existence serves as a deterrent. Muslim integration must be a priority. The present state of affairs where such a sizeable population feels excluded from the national mainstream, is neither good for the country's social stability nor does it make economic sense. For, ultimately, an unproductive community of 170 million people is a drag on the entire nation's resources.

However, while helping Muslim upliftment and integration, the government should stop appeasing Muslim fundamentalism if it wants the community to progress. There should be no more Shah Banos again. In India there is a slightly different notion of secularism, with the state actively promoting the right to practice religion, than in the west where the state keeps itself at arm's length from religion. But even by Indian standards, it should not mean pandering to the worst sectarian instincts. The policy of competitive appeasement of Hindu and Muslim fundamentalism has already done enough damage to the country's social fabric, and unless we want to see it ripped apart completely, there is no justification for carrying on with this lunacy. At a time when a new generation of Muslims is trying to free the community from the fundamentalist stranglehold and give it a fresh start, any hint of hugging the mullahs either by political parties, the government, or the media will tantamount to a betrayal of Muslim interests for which history will never forgive us.

Part II

In Their Own Words

RAAZIA SIDDIQUI (28) works for a multinational corporation

'Aap special hongi, varna yahan discrimination toh hota hi hai!' (You must be special. Otherwise everyone faces discrimination here.)

An elderly Muslim made this statement while I was sharing my experiences at a gathering and happened to mention that the idea of discrimination was unreal, and that I had never experienced it all my life. I was stunned for a while, both by the irrationality of the argument and by the abruptness of the interruption. I took a moment to reflect on the gentleman's disapproval of my stand on discrimination and the 'special' status that had been bestowed upon me.

The interruption was a learning experience for me. It was a demonstration of the negative mindset with which our community, at present, is grappling. I failed to understand how without even knowing about my life, he made such a sweeping remark. I was not 'special', I had worked hard—spending countless nights and days in strife.

Being a senior person, why did he fail to offer a word of advice or share a lesson from his life's experience that we, as youth, could have benefitted from? Was it not incumbent upon him and the other elderly Muslims to keep behind their negative experiences and ensure that their negativity is not disseminated to our generation, so that we learn to co-exist in peace and harmony, and are able to optimally utilize the available opportunities? When I could understand this, why could he not?

Discrimination, to my mind, is the phenomenon of turning a blind eye to reality. By doing so, we fail to identify our shortcomings and fail to course-correct our life. This is just one example of a negative outlook to life. I would not shy away from confessing that the negative thinking of our community has cost us dearly. Today we find ourselves enmeshed in problems, and are unable to find a solution. Muslim media, our leaders and our congregations, all disseminate ideas not worth owning. It is unfortunate that the people of my community cannot recognize that it is merit and not favouritism which eventually leads one to success. No one can complain about the dearth of opportunities because we live in a world of unlimited possibilities. Post-globalization, opportunities have increased manifold. Institutions only look for the right attitude and sincerity in individuals. I have never come across a meritorious and diligent Muslim who has not progressed. It is not a case of discrimination; it is a case of working hard, working diligently, and keeping oneself away from negative thoughts of all kinds. Unfortunately, Muslims have remained so archaic in their approach that they become a case of missed opportunities.

It was the responsibility of the elders to instill in our generation the aspiration to attain best education and excel in whatever we do. This would have sufficed for the young Muslims to climb the ladder of success. Unfortunately, this did not happen. Partly the blame lies on our elders, who did not guide us by means of informal education, and partly on us, who would rather garner knowledge of all that was frivolous.

In my opinion, we are not discriminated against, on the contrary, Muslims *are the ones who discriminate*; by living in self-glory and pride, they consider themselves above all the rest.

Born in a traditional Muslim family, I soon became a practicing Muslim. Though I was following the religion blindly, the practices had become a part of my daily schedule. These practices defined my religious identity and my notions were moulded by my limited understanding of what I thought was religion.

Our conscience raises questions about all the things that we observe and sense. Unfortunately, as we grow up, partly because of ignorance and partly under social pressures, we tend to suppress the questions that arise in our mind. Nature, however, continues to impart lessons—sometimes through others' experiences and sometimes through our own. I was still in school when America was stormed on 9/11. I still vividly remember seeing the images and videos of the destruction the so-called jihadis had caused. I felt so totally miserable that I detested being a Muslim. I did not like being a part of congregations that would discuss the aftermath of these attacks. I was disillusioned.

I spent some years in this struggle until my journey to explore Islam began. My learning continues even today but I must confess, that during this journey, my belief and my religious sensibilities have undergone a complete transformation. I realized that Islam and present-day Muslims were different from each other. Neither was an introduction of the other. Islam, to my disbelief, was a religion where peace was considered the *summum bonum* (greatest or supreme good). It gave paramount importance to intellectual development of man, sanctioned equal respect for man and woman, encouraged man to be a rational thinker, and focused on discovering the being called God. I was at peace.

I learnt that Islam focuses on harnessing the true potential of man and developing in him God-oriented spirit, which then manifests itself in the form of practice. It urges man to develop high character and live harmoniously and contribute to society. As such, there is no need for us as Muslims to find a distinct identity for ourselves. We must focus on finding common ground, and assimilate within the society to learn from each other, and together grow as human beings.

I learnt that the true basis of Islam can only be Quran and Hadith. There is no other yardstick to evaluate one's decision. Anyone who would study the Quran would realize that those who talk in the language of *jihad* or violence and try to spread negativity can never base their arguments on the Islamic criterion.

In my opinion, the problem with our community is that we do not judge what we hear on the basis of the Quran and Hadith. Unfortunately, most of us do not even know what is written in the Quran because all our lives we only recite its verses without feeling the need to understand its meaning. Most of us are unaware of the fact that our religion urges us to evaluate everything on rational grounds, and so, without raising a single question, we succumb to the emotional speeches and irrational commandments of the present-day leaders, and offer ourselves to be a part of the herd.

Behind the Veil

The topic of the conversation was Hijab in Islam. Stressing on its importance, a youth cited that he had been told that Islam ordains women to be confined to their homes so that they are not seen by men outside their household. My family never forced me to wear a veil. Were they doing something wrong and beyond the realms of the religious framework? During the Prophet's time, Muslim women were active in different fields such as agriculture, horticulture and social work. But at the same time they constantly preserved their feminine character. In the early history of Islam there are many such incidents which show that a woman has equal freedom as man. In this respect there is no difference between the two. Islamic literature mentions some pious women who have played highly creative roles in their society, like Hajira, the wife of the Prophet Abraham; Mariam, the mother of Jesus; Khadija and Aishah, the wives of the Prophet of Islam. These women, accepted as models in the society of believers, are good examples for the women of today.

At present, Muslims use the term 'hijab' as equivalent to 'burqa' but the word hijab is not used in the Quran in this sense. History shows that the burqa was a part of the culture of Persia. When Islam entered Persia, a complete civilisation was already in existence there. Under the influence of the Iranian culture, the burqa was adopted by Muslims. Gradually, it became a part of Muslim culture.

It gives me immense strength to realize that the religion of Islam focuses on spirit rather than on form. It lays emphasis on pious thinking and value-based character. According to Islam, Muslims must purify themselves in terms of ethics. Muslim men and women must develop themselves in terms of spirituality. Women must play a constructive role in the society rather than become mere objects of entertainment.

Muslim Concerns

I strongly believe that learning is the key to all kinds of success. It is the only ladder to all kinds of progress. With learning, all else follows; without learning, there is much to lose. In my opinion therefore lack of good education is one of the biggest issues faced by the Muslim community at large. This includes both formal and informal education. While formal education prepares a child for the competitive world, informal education inculcates morals and develops within him a pragmatic and introspective approach to life. This is what makes him a responsible citizen of the country.

While Muslim families have begun the process to ensure that their children get formal education, they still have to work hard on first understanding the importance of informal education and then imparting it to their next generation. This would mean giving up the psyche of discrimination. It is our inability to do so until now which has held us back from progressing. We should stop feeling insecure and pragmatically think of finding a solution to our problems. We should singularly focus on education and keep ourselves away from all kinds of negative emotions. But it must be borne in mind that any kind of development is a slow process. This process of being singularly focused on development will have to continue for generations, and only then will we see the fruits being reaped.

I would also like to discuss the issue of reservation for Muslims. Personally, I have never been able to reconcile to the idea of reservation because, in my opinion, easy access to resources discourages growth and development of an individual, and a community at large. It is only when there is struggle, strife and a will to succeed in the world of competition that the best abilities within an individual are realized. We have several examples of people who, while they were from modest households with meagre means, managed to reach the very top of their field by virtue of their diligence and sincerity. The former President of India Dr A.P.J. Abdul Kalam is a case in point. While reservation may seem alluring initially, it only renders the foundation hollow and is a toxic development.

Another concern emanating from the feeling of insecurity is the ghetto mentality of Muslims. We do not realize that by doing so we are restricting our own growth and development. Exchange of views in a diverse atmosphere is the best means of developing ideas. Unfortunately, Muslims have alienated themselves on their own—their reactionary approach and complaining attitude are some of the attributes that make them appear inhospitable and averse to intellectual development. Be it a fatwa or a supposed act of irreverence, the Muslim youth does not take a moment to get ignited. I experienced this myself on many occasions, more recently at the Jaipur Literature Festival 2012, which again made it to the headlines on account of vehement Muslim opposition to Salman Rushdie's visit to India.

For the sake of argument, even if I agree that one must respond to such issues, my question is: Why, instead of taking to the streets, can we not respond academically? Why do we prove each time that we are highly volatile and inflammable? Such an approach is a result of lack of understanding of Islam. If we had understood Islam, the first lesson we would have learnt would be patience, piety and peaceful coexistence. The Quran, and examples from the life of Prophet Muhammad, abound in these teachings, if only we would take a lesson from them.

Generation Next

The new generation, in my opinion, is becoming increasingly disinterested in the way religion is thrust upon them. We are no longer satisfied with only 'what'; we want to know the 'why' as well. But because the families are conditioned in a certain way, they are not able to give a rational explanation to address young minds. As a result, youngsters are growing averse to religion, which, if rightly understood, can be the most powerful guiding ideology in the life of an individual.

Today we are exposed to a wide variety of media and other forms of interactive experience sharing which has put us amidst a jungle of ideas. We have seen conflicts in the name of religion, and the results of it as well. Some of us have started to assume that religion separates. Neither do conventional explanations appeal to such minds nor do the dictates of clerics affect their lifestyle anymore. This is a very serious situation. In my opinion, it is an extremely crucial period, one that may cause a turnaround of the outlook of our generations, but this would happen only if those in responsible positions assess the situation correctly and rise to the need of the hour.

It must be recognized that the situation has changed and so have the sensitivities of people. All of us have seen what negative ideas and propagation of violence leads to. Be it Kashmir or Gujarat or America, the Muslim youth is increasingly becoming tired of the same old stories from the past—the psyche of hatred and the result of violence that they have witnessed. These occurrences have made most of us disillusioned.

There is need for a complete overhaul of ideas and for the true face of Islam to be made known to the new generations—a religion based on rationality, peace and love for humanity, which will become their guiding beacon in these tumultuous times.

The questions being raised by the young must be answered so that they are guided. If this happens, the generations to come will find the right direction to exist peacefully and harmoniously in this country. If, however, our elders fail to do so, it will have disastrous results. Today, if I take my own example, I have consciously chosen to practice Islam. It is the peaceful nature of Islam which attracted me to it. Islam seeks its proponents to lead a life of reflection, introspection and to constantly develop their intellect. In it, I found rational explanation of my existential questions. Because of being guided, I could discover the true face of Islam, which helped me dispel notions and myths about the religion.

In retrospect, religion, to me, was nothing but blind faith. Contrary to my notion, I was astonished to learn that the study of human history reveals that it was actually Islam that ushered in the modern age. In fact, I was surprised to learn that the acclaimed historian, Arnold Toynbee, has acknowledged that the prolonged age of nature worship and superstitions was actually put an end to, for the first time, by the universal monotheistic revolution brought about by Islam. My mind could not fathom the contradiction of what I saw in the society, my own notions, and what my study revealed. I kept asking myself the question: How is it that the present-day Muslims, who are the followers of that same Islam which taught science to the whole world in its initial stages, are at present lagging far behind others in scientific education, and have become enveloped in superstitions themselves?

I got my answer in the writings of Maulana Wahiduddin Khan, a noted Islamic scholar. According to him, because of being involved in political pursuits, Muslims did not pay adequate importance to scientific education. They did little or nothing to set up an infrastructure for its dissemination. By the time the Muslim leaders realized, it was quite late. Muslims had already lagged behind in terms of receiving modern scientific education. This explains why Muslims today no longer think scientifically. This lack of scientific temperament has served as a major obstacle in the path of intellectual development of the Muslim community.

Future of Muslims in India

India is a land of opportunities. Being a melting pot of cultures, it embraces every one and allows them to flourish and unveil their potential. Our future, I feel, is the brightest in our country—the only condition being that we change our outlook and become positive thinkers.

There are over fifty Muslim countries in the world but the situation in each of them is not hidden from the world. Nowhere are Muslims as free to express their thoughts and ideas as they are in India. Be it the educational infrastructure, the health services set up, or any other amenity, India suffices for all our needs.

Not only is India home to a number of multinational companies, it is also one of the fastest growing economies of our time. We must be thankful for being born in a democracy like India, which provides complete freedom of expression and provides unlimited avenues to grow and develop.

I have been asked many times the question: Did I ever feel discriminated against? My answer is a clear and an unambiguous: 'No'. I have never felt discriminated against in my country. I have grown to realize that hard work never goes waste. If one is sincere and diligent in one's approach to gather knowledge and excel in one's field of work, the sky is the limit. I would like to add here that discrimination is not a factual occurrence, it is a state of mind. Those who complain of such an occurrence do not analyse their own mistakes.

The Quran urges its proponents to evaluate their own mistakes and introspect rather than put the blame on others. It propagates a culture of blaming thyself which teaches one to reflect upon one's own deficiencies and assume responsibility for what did not go right. In doing so, one would achieve two-fold benefits—on the one hand, acceptance of reality will make one a pragmatic thinker, and on the other hand, one will save oneself from being negative and will be able to develop oneself so as to recognize other potential opportunities that may be realized.

When the American politician Daniel Webster was told that he mustn't join the legal profession for it was already overcrowded, he said: 'There is always room at the top.' This is a fact. Primarily because every corporation and every institution seeks people who are sincere, and are able to outperform and excel. The fourth Caliph, Ali, said: 'Value of a man lies in excellence.' Striving for excellence is a virtue, which is what leads man to the top.

In my interactions with most Muslims I have realized that because of being trapped in the psyche of negative thinking and complaint, we have completely lost sight of a positive tomorrow. Slightest of provocation is sufficient to arouse our emotions and make us commit unworthy acts. Because most of us only recite the Quran and do not understand it, we remain unaware about the Quranic formula for successful living. According to it, 'Surely with every hardship, there is ease'. (94:5-6)

This verse changed my outlook towards life. It tells man that God has made this world such that problems are accompanied with opportunities so that man can avail them and reach a positive outcome. However, recognizing opportunities is not an easy task. It requires immense patience and courage to be able to overcome all the emotional inducements and focus energies on identifying and tapping the opportunities that abound in our world. I pray that we are able to course correct and convert our potential into actual, before it is too late.

SANA RASHID SIDDIQUI (35), IT professional

These days, Muslims are categorised either as Islamists or moderates. Though I would like to believe that I am simply a Muslim, the general perception of the world around me would categorise me as a moderate Muslim. I follow the five pillars of Islam with conviction. However, I do not wear hijab nor do I claim to be an expert on Hadith or Quran. I do not drink or smoke, but have no problem with those who do. I completed my primary education in Libya and higher studies in Aligarh. As a result, I grew up in a comfortable Islamic environment throughout my formative years. Being born in a well-educated and cultured Muslim family, the basic teaching of Islam—i.e. humanity—was ingrained in us since the very beginning. It is this fundamental foundation of humanity that has helped build a much stronger personality and belief which remain unaffected by threats of any kind.

After my marriage I moved to New Delhi with my husband, and started exploring job options in the field of writing. Many of my friends and acquaintances had warned me that it would be extremely difficult for me to succeed in such a competitive city as Delhi, especially as a Muslim coming from Aligarh. However, after a decade as a successful professional in Delhi, my belief that talent and conviction are the two most important qualities that one needs to possess to succeed anywhere has grown stronger. Being a Muslim in India, I am well aware and conscious of my own religious identity and possess a sense of complete belonging towards my motherland. When my friends and acquaintances from other communities pose certain questions related to my religion, I willingly try to clear certain misconceptions related to Islam, and try to present to them the real, tolerant image of Muslims.

Many of my Muslim relatives and friends have adopted two extreme paths, especially post Ayodhya, 9/11, and the Gujarat riots, etc. I see in most of them a conscious effort to shed the orthodox Muslim image and, in the process, they tend to lose their own Muslim identities. The other extreme comprises Muslims who consciously try to show off and impose their religious identities by wearing hijab and growing a beard. However, it is the moderate Muslims who continue to be acceptable by all others while the extremely orthodox ones tend to lose acceptance within their own community.

Young Muslims are more tolerant, more sure of their identities and have realised the importance of coexisting peacefully among all other communities. We are making conscious efforts to mix with other communities instead of being confined to our own. There is a heightened sense of patriotism and rightful belonging among young Muslims in India. There is an increased sense of pride in being Indian Muslims, and the earlier attitude of sympathising or empathising with Pakistani Muslims just because they belong to the same community, has almost been discarded (starkly evident in the India-Pakistan matches).

Therefore, in today's extremely competitive and real world, being an Indian Muslim is no different than being an Indian Hindu, Sikh, Christian, or Parsi. The need of the hour for young Muslims is to find acceptance and success with their religious identities intact instead of shedding their religious beliefs to find acceptance and success. Young Muslims need to realise that a liberal outlook does not require us to discard the basic teachings of Islam. In fact, they should accept the truth that our religion basically teaches us to be good human beings; and in serving people well, we serve God well. A couplet by the famous Urdu Poet Allama Iqbal aptly conveys the dilemma of today's young Muslims in India:

Zahidey tang nazar ne mujhey kaafir jaana,
Aur kaafir samajhta hai musalmaan hoon main!

(The insolent cleric labelled me a kaafir (unbeliever),
yet the kaafir considers me a Muslim!)

MEHER REHMAN (37), development activist and founder of Taamir India Foundation which works on women's educational and health issues

Being an educated and progressive Muslim professional and living in a metropolitan city means belonging to a totally different context in contemporary India. This context, much as I have experienced it, is more accepting, individual centred, materialistic, very competent, and driven by opportunities where one's cultural and religious background does not matter on a day to day basis. It has similar rules and norms for everyone, largely, and everyone shares the challenges and constraints that an urban context confronts them with. However, things are different in the smaller towns and rural parts of the country where one's economic status, caste and religious faith determine how they get treated in the society. My Muslim friends who live in the second rung cities or smaller towns have faced various degree of hostilities and discriminations on account of being a Muslim. Essentially, the overall current political environment in India is a constant reminder of the growing anti-Islam sentiment as well as an extremist Hindutva ideology which certainly impacts the psyche of all Muslims, irrespective of where they reside in the country.

The demolition of Babri Masjid, the 2002 state-sponsored carnage of Muslims in Gujarat, and the global impact of 9/11 have affected the Muslim psyche in the country, and definitely made people like me—the so-called liberal educated Muslim elite—more conscious about our identity. This has played out both ways. It has resulted in the younger generation of Muslims either becoming too religious and conscious of projecting their faith, or totally distancing themselves from religion. For someone like me, I feel I am now more open and wanting to say it loud and clear that I am a Muslim. In fact, now I feel a greater need and a sense of responsibility to put it out there that there is also an educated face of the Muslims who have a profound association with their faith, but who do not identify themselves with the image created by radical Muslims. To perform and do well in my profession as well as my civic life holds much more meaning to me now than ever before.

I believe that a trust deficit does exist among the Muslims in India and this cuts across age groups and geographies. Our faith in the law makers and the law enforcers is pretty weak, which is definitely not a healthy indicator. Personally, I'm always very apprehensive when I have to interact with a police officer or an Immigration Officer at the Delhi airport since I know his interaction with me would be based on his prejudices about my faith. Further, as the younger generation of Muslims we do have doubts about our future role and security in the Indian polity to a great extent, especially when our loyalty towards our country gets questioned. Interestingly, for my generation who has grown up in India, along with this trepidation exists a parallel sense of belonging towards this country, and a good level of faith in the democratic system of our governance and spirit of secularism that still holds strong in the people.

We have to share some part of the blame for our current condition too. The reality of Muslims in India after independence is that there has been a clear lack of a strong, coherent and intelligent leadership. The community's need for better education, improved economic opportunities, social justice, greater engagement with the local governance and democratic processes mostly remain unaddressed. This outcome is not just critical for the welfare of the Muslim community in India but for the development of the country as a whole. This is definitely worrisome since even six years after the Sachar Committee report highlighted huge gaps and constraints, nothing much has been done. The Prime Minister's New 15-Point Programme for Welfare of Minorities announced in 2005 has still not been rolled out in its true spirit. Unfortunately, even today, there are not enough Muslim role models or young leaders in mainstream Indian politics to give the much needed impetus to Muslim development.

I would agree that despite all these challenges there is a new mood among Muslims in India, pioneered by young Muslims who, despite their obsession with their Muslim identity and pull towards religiosity, are more integrated, confident and have a sense of belonging to India than some of the previous generations. There is also a greater willingness among them to introspect rather than blame others for all their problems. I feel that this positive development in the attitude of the young Muslims needs to be reciprocated with an equally encouraging response from the Government, else it may be a short-lived one with serious repercussions for the country as a whole in the years to come.

SADIA KHAN (26), research scholar, Jamia Millia Islamia, New Delhi

'I am glad my parents returned to India. My father left for Kuwait in the '60s and I would have hated growing up in the Middle East. Frankly, as a Muslim I would choose to be in India rather than in any other country of the world,' says Suhail Baghdadi, a marketing consultant from Mumbai.

'Pakistanis think that Muslims in India are living a shoddy life. I think it's the opposite! I would definitely not like to be in Pakistan. It's in a total mess,' says Ayaz Matin, a management trainee. These words of Suhail and Ayaz express the mood of the young Muslim when it comes to living in India. And it is not without its reasons. India offers the essential ingredients for positive, constructive activities. Brimming with opportunities, it proffers to its citizens freedom of all kinds.

Moreover, the majority of Indians follow Hinduism, a religion which proclaims that all paths lead to the truth or the same destination. It would therefore not be an exaggeration to say that Hindus are a singularly tolerant people. Living among a tolerant people, in a secular democratic country, and in a nation with a spiritual heritage, is surely a blessing.

Suhail narrates: 'A Pakistani acquaintance once asked me what it was like being a Muslim and to have a Shiv Sena government in Maharashtra, in the year 1992. My immediate reaction was that for the first time I had not seen a police van outside the mosque during Friday prayers. To which he remarked that there were cops outside mosques in Pakistan irrespective of which government was in power!'

According to the British historian, Arnold Toynbee, development is a product of what he calls the 'challenge-response mechanism'. To him, a community that faces challenge gradually emerges as a 'creative community'. In view of this, Muslims in India are in an incredibly advantageous position. In India they have a challenge from the majority community and this challenge provides a guarantee of their unending development. Challenge enhances creativity, and creativity leads to success. Challenge unfolds one's potential, and this situation for Indian Muslims is very much in evidence.

A simple comparison of the Muslim condition in 1947 to that of today, is revealing. That Muslims in India are progressing by leaps and bounds so that their future is indeed bright, is evident in the example of the residential colony, Nizamuddin West, where I live. Immigrants from Pakistan built Nizamuddin West, an upscale locality of New Delhi, after the partition of India. Muslims in the colony were at the time few and far between. But today Muslims make up more than 70 per cent of the colony. Being able to buy property in an area such as Nizamuddin is one of the many examples that reflect the economic progress Muslims have made since 1947.

However, commenting on the situation of the Muslims today, Maulana Wahiduddin Khan, a noted Islamic scholar and founder of the Centre for Peace and Spirituality International, says, 'India is progressing and so are Muslims. However, Muslims have not been able to progress as much as the opportunities allow.' This, he thinks, is because of the negative thinking of Muslims. The concern of the Muslim today is economic progress and though he has achieved much, he can do much better if he adopts positive thinking. So, the progress is not due to an intellectual awakening among Muslims but is due rather to social compulsions.

The Muslim reaction to the participation of Salman Rushdie in the Jaipur Literature Festival 2012 is testimony to the intolerance rampant among Muslims. Not only was Rushdie's participation cancelled, his video talk was later cancelled too. A Muslim protester said: 'Rivers of blood will flow here if they show Rushdie' (The *Times of India*, 25 January 2012).

The main reason for this negativity and intolerance in the case of Muslims is paranoia. Muslims, after the advent of Islam, established an empire which lasted for many centuries. So Muslim history became a political history, and the Muslim psyche a political psyche. But, after the advent of colonialism, they suddenly found that they had lost their empire. Muslims today live in their political memories. That is, they live in past glory.

Theodore Paul Wright Jr divides the Indian Muslims into two broad categories—the 'coastal' Muslims and the 'inland' Muslims. The latter he calls 'monument-conscious, living in the midst of their Taj Mahals and Red Forts and Char Minars'— those who have not forgotten that they once constituted the ruling elite minority. Therefore, if Muslims fail to relate to their present situation, it is in large measure due to their glorious past.

If Muslims abandoned negative thinking, and concentrated on availing of the opportunities in India, they would soon become a giver community and not a taker community. An apt example is the Parsi community of India. Barely a hundred thousand, their case is that of cultural individuality, yet it does not distance them from the national mainstream. Neither do they demand nor do they protest. With industrial success, they enjoy a fame and status out of all proportion to their numbers.

Not only is the economic growth of Muslims evident but also the Muslim mind today has undergone a noticeable change. Muslim thinking of the post-independence era was shaped by the writings of personalities such as the early twentieth century poet, Akbar Allahabadi. Condemning modern education, he writes: *Hum aise kul kitaben qaabil-e-zabti samajhte hain; ke jin ko padh ke bete, baap ko khabtee samajhte hain.* (I consider all such books worthy of ban after reading which children think that their parents are stupid.)

The young Muslim, on the other hand, is questioning the old thinking. The example of Mohammad Ziaullah is illustrative. Zia holds a degree of alimiat from Nadwatul Ulama, Lucknow, one of the most prestigious institutions of Islamic learning in India. But today he is a research scholar at the Jawaharlal Nehru University, New Delhi. Once out of the Islamic seminary, he says, he felt he was a 'misfit, unprepared for the life outside the educational institution. I realized that something was missing, that something important was missing. So I enrolled myself at the American Centre of Language, Lucknow. When I was able to read books in English, I realized that there was so much more to be learnt. Later on at Jawaharlal Nehru University, I discovered a new world. At Nadwa, I had just one perspective of the world; at JNU I discovered the other. Unlike the madrasa, JNU had a culture of debate and discussion. Had I not come here, I would have been incomplete.'

The Muslim leaders are clearly responsible for the intellectual backwardness of Muslims today. Another trend, which caused Muslims to distance themselves from modern education, was the questioning by the young of the age-old traditions and dogma. It was observed that though the older generation adhered to the tenets of religion, the young would not follow unexplained phenomena. Unable to address the modern mind, they declared modern education insalubrious. Abul Ala Maududi, for example, calls institutions of modern education the new age 'slaughter houses'.

The Muslim Identity

Islam requires one to maintain one's identity, not in terms of culture but in terms of character. And that character should be marked by such moral values as truthfulness, patience, tolerance, pacifism, positive thinking, well-wishing for all and freedom from hatred. These are the values that make up the unique identity of a Muslim.

It is worth noting that the term 'identity' is not found in the Islamic scriptures—the Quran and Hadith. For the scriptures, it is an alien term. If Muslims wish to adopt a particular identity in terms of their dress, they are free to do so; however, that will be their cultural identity and not Islamic identity. Cultural identity has no Islamic importance.

Often what is external, such as the hijab or a beard, are considered by Muslims important elements of a Muslim's identity. The hijab and beard among Indian Muslims are not new phenomena, however. It is a fact that in the pre-independent days there were more hijab users and bearded men. This was largely an outcome of the two-nation theory championed by Muhammad Iqbal, Muhammad Ali Jinnah and others. The two-nation theory was the ideology that the primary identity of Muslims on the Indian subcontinent is their religion, rather than their language or ethnicity.

The present situation therefore is nothing but a remnant of the past. Muslims therefore would wear a hijab or flaunt a beard not because they wished them to be the markers of their identity but as a matter of following a long tradition. Moreover, the present day is witness to a rapid erosion in this tradition, evident in the words of Suhail: 'The region that you come from defines and shapes your identity more than your religion. Also, I don't wish to wear my religion on my sleeve.'

The identity of a community is generally determined by cultural elements rather than a particular religion. In the age of land-based nationhood, it is for Muslims to adopt the same identity as that of their other co-patriots.

If one were to look at the image of the Indian Muslims in the media, one would most likely form a negative opinion, but what is reported in the media are few and far between instances. The majority, one will discover, is quite different from the media picture; the concern of this people is to receive quality education and to meet the challenge of competition.

My family belongs to the district Azamgarh of U.P. After independence this district was considered one of the backward districts of India. But that is not the case today. Swept by a gradual change, English schools have opened up in almost every village. Mostly those Muslims who became aware of the importance of education have established these schools, and here the students are mostly Muslim. A stark example is found in the remote village of Badharia. From this village hailed the businessman Shakeel Khan, who established there the Ziauddin

Khan Memorial School. The astonishing change was perhaps best expressed by Saleem Shervani, former Minister of State for External Affairs: 'One can hardly believe seeing an institution like the Ziauddin Khan Memorial School in a rural area.'

According to Delhi-based journalist Rana Ayyub, recipient of the prestigious Sanskriti Award 2011: 'In the last five years the image of Muslims vis-à-vis the media has changed quite a bit. Today, no one is surprised if a Muslim is progressive, if a Muslim has broken barriers. The Muslim society has moved out of the syndrome of being victims. For example, of the five awardees of the Sanskriti Award last year, four were Muslims. Had this been the case earlier the media would have extensively covered it, but today it is an everyday happening; Muslims are progressing and are in every field. I was not identified as a Muslim who received the award.'

Of the many events one that stands out in the recent history of Indian Muslims is the Babri Masjid issue. Babri Masjid was built four hundred years ago. According to the historical account, it was a controversial construction from the very beginning because the mosque was built adjacent to what is called the Ram Chabutra. Since the Ram Chabutra is as holy as a temple for the Hindus, after the independence of India, some sections of the Hindus wished to build it.

With this, Muslims were led into a position where they could write a new chapter in the history of India that Hindus and Muslims can live in India with a great sense of brotherhood. It was possible for Muslims to set a tradition, a very powerful tradition that no difference whatsoever can disrupt Hindu-Muslim unity. Muslims could have played a non-controversial role by simply relocating the mosque. Moreover, the construction of the Babri Masjid does not follow the Islamic principle that two places of worship should be at a stone's throw distance; this was an additional reason why Muslims should have opted for the relocation of the mosque. But Muslims failed to adopt this line of action.

The demolition of Babri Masjid was a sad event in the history of India. But today the Indian Muslim seems to have forgotten the issue. Now, if one conducts a survey regarding the Ayodhya tragedy, one will find that it remains in the Muslim mind only as a faint memory.

An evidence of this fact is that some self-styled Muslim leaders have repeatedly given calls to commemorate Babri Masjid day on December 6 every year. But this call remains unanswered. It is a fact that now issues of such kind are not the concern of Indian Muslims. Muslims, now, are engaged in constructive fields. The peaceful reception of the Supreme Court verdict on the Babri Masjid issue is a testimony to this fact.

The Way Ahead

Some people are born with a silver spoon in their mouth. There are the haves, and the have-nots. But this does not mean that the have-nots remain so. Take the former president of India, Dr A.P.J. Abdul Kalam. Dr Kalam was born into a poor family. His parents were unable to pay his school fee but, in the latter part of his life, he rose to the highest position in the country; he became the President of India. This means that the haves and have-nots equation is wrong. It is better to categorize people as 'potential haves' and 'actual haves'. When Dr Kalam was born, he was a member of the 'potential haves' category but, at a later stage, he became a member of the 'actual haves' category.

The fact is that every man and woman is born with great potential but it lies dormant. In this sense everyone belongs to the 'potential haves' category. If he is able to activate his capacity, and he is able to plan his life, he is bound to become a member of the 'actual haves' category.

But when Muslims complain, they become blind to this fact. For example, when a Muslim fails to acquire a job, he often complains that the cause of his unemployment is the M (Muslim) factor. In other words, bias against Muslims. Such thinking is against the spirit of the age where the Q (Quality) Factor is the most important.

We live in the age of competition. Those in need of employees cannot afford the policy of discrimination. In this highly competitive world, they know they cannot survive if they do not provide quality. So, if they find someone who has good professional skills, they are compelled to hire him in their own interest. In such a world, anyone who complains about discrimination is simply saying that in terms of professional skills he is not a good choice!

Ayaz Matin, a management trainee, says: 'If one finds oneself in an unpleasant situation, one must not blame the system but do something about it. I think education is the way to uplift ourselves. To succeed in anything, we need to learn the rules of the game, and then, perform. We cannot say nobody invited us to play the game.'

It is unfortunate that there are many people in this world who cannot or will not recognize an opportunity when it comes their way. Frederick Langbridge observed: 'Two men looked out from the prison bars, one saw the mud and the other saw stars.'

So if a class or community which considers itself disadvantaged or deprived goes through life seeing only the mud and never the stars, there is little hope of it making progress, with or without external encouragement. Considering that Indian Muslims seem to have spent a very long time concentrating their attention on the mud and doing very little in reaching for the stars, it is time now that they had a rethink.

SABA MAHMOOD BASHIR (37), writer, lecturer

Those were the months of August and September 1992. The kar sewaks were gathering momentum. I was in the 11th standard in Allahabad, Uttar Pradesh. As long as I was reading about the background of the Babri Masjid turmoil in the newspapers, it was a piece of news, a concern of the entire nation but did not involve me directly. As a young girl of 15-16 years, with my upbringing with a set of educated parents and grand-parents, my identity remained that of an Indian only. Till one day, while I was sitting in the class and we heard slogans of Jai Sri Ram, as some kar sewaks crossed the school. One of my friends, sitting next to me, started boasting how her family was sending food every evening to the sewaks gathered in Allahabad or to those who were on their way to Ayodhya, stopping abruptly to realise that I was a Muslim.

It was at that moment that I realised I was a Muslim, and somehow different from the rest in the class. Having studied in a Convent there were only one or two Muslims in each class, and we were different. Felt that too, at times, but never distant from the rest—that is, until 1992.

My parents, both my mother and father, were born in independent India, in other words, post Partition, where their respective parents had chosen to stay. However, my maternal grandmother had been a witness to the partition massacre from close quarters, and actually survived through dead bodies. In spite of that, at the riots that followed post the Babri Masjid-Ayodhya turmoil, she pointed out to me, 'Your generation was ignorant of the killings, what we had gone through. These riots, post Babri Masjid demolition, will recreate a scar, which will again take a long time to go'. There was a sigh in her voice, which remained with me. There was something in her sigh which made me think. Her tone still lingers in my mind. And the Babri Masjid demolition did become a watershed in the Muslim minds in India.

The identity of being a Muslim was always imposed from the 'outside'! As in, we never had discussions about religion in our homes, and were always taught that all religions are equal. All Gods are the same. I was seven or eight when my first cousin married a Hindu. The marriage was accepted within the family. However, dealing with the society was a different thing altogether. About two decades later, I think the situation has only worsened.

Even today, when someone else looks at me, they look at me as a Muslim first and then an Indian, a woman, an educator, etc. etc. A couple of years back, I was regularly getting calls from NDTV for Barkha Dutt's programme *We the People* to be part of the audience. Everytime I got the call I would be informed that it was a Muslim issue. Be it Imrana's case or any other. After a couple of calls, I lost my cool and scolded the girl on the telephone and wrote a stinker to the channel—'Why is it that I do not get a call when you wish to discuss the education policy of the county? Why are my ideas only required when it is a Muslim issue? Why am I always looked at as a Muslim?' I am a woman, an educated one, and a working one too, with a little daughter. I can jolly well discuss other pertinent issues of the country. I did get a call for another issue but, needless to say, I was offended by the media by then and did not go. In continuation to the idea of identifications, when 'others' look at me as a Muslim, calling me Mohamaddan many a times, there are Muslims as well who want to put you in compartments. I have always been asked the question if I am a Sunni or a Shia. I learned this lesson early in life. My father is a Shia and my mother a Sunni. I learned my namaz with my mother so I offer the Sunni namaz and my younger brother learned it with my father so he offers the Shia namaz. Even during the Ramzan, ammi and I would start our Iftaar while abbu and my brother would wait, looking at their watches. (Shias open their fast about 10 minutes after the Sunni's, though, personally I do not understand the logic). We grew up in a family where ritualistic Islam was not important. However, I feel, people like us are in a minority. In the last decade, especially post the Gujarat carnage, there is a distinct rise in the ritualistic religion. Last year I joined Jamia Millia Islamia as a Guest Faculty. For about two months I was given a substitution to teach General English to BA (Honours in Islamic Studies), second year. My first reaction was that of irritation as the front row was occupied by 'ninja turtles' (I heard this phrase from an activist and an educationist, for women who do purdah in a way that only the eyes are seen)! Anyways, taking it up as a challenge, I went ahead with the classes—with the sole aim that I would surely open one small vent in at least a couple of students. The story that we were reading was O'Henry's *The Gift of Magi*, the background being that of Christmas. I was rather shocked to discover that hardly any student knew about the customs related with the festival. I kept on questioning them, if they had seen the festivity associated with Christmas, or for that matter with Diwali too, only to be disappointed further. Till a young student, gallantly, and aggressively, got up to tell me, 'Why will we wish anyone Diwali or eat sweets, it is not our festival?' I wanted to know how it was affecting their religion by participating in someone's festival. As expected, I did not get a satisfactory answer. Anyway, I was happy with the answer that I gave them, 'You need to strengthen your faith in your religion if it gets threatened by eating sweets on Diwali and Christmas'. I could see shock in the eyes of some, an effort to comprehend what I had just said, in others. There were, at least two, who kind of agreed with what I had pointed out. Maybe I was successful in opening at least one window in a closed mind.

NASIR ZAIDI (37), businessman

Let me make it clear at the outset that I never saw any conflict in being an Indian and a Muslim at the same time. I have a religious identity as a Muslim and a national identity as an Indian—and I am equally proud of both. I find it insulting when I am asked whether I am an 'Indian first or a Muslim first'. It is a mischievous question. It is meant to sow seeds of suspicion about Muslims' 'Indian-ness'. I've stopped answering this question because I don't want to dignify it with an answer. India is my country. It is the only place where I feel comfortable. It is home.

I have strong views on religious extremism. Those who have hijacked Islam for their own agendas are its worst enemies. They are on the wrong road. It is because of them that Muslims have got such a negative image. People think that every Muslim is a raving fundamentalist mullah. That is far from true.

I am a practicing Muslim. But I don't impose my view on others. I have a beard but my wife doesn't wear a hijab. I respect her decision. Who am I to force it on her? But there are fundamentalists who want to impose their own interpretation of Islam on everyone. That's dangerous. There are Muslims who are not particularly religious but that doesn't make them lesser Muslims. It is not for me to judge who is a good Muslim.

Tolerance is the essence of Islam. It doesn't teach coercion. Yet we have become so intolerant, thanks to a brand of Islam propagated by the Saudis. They have taken the soul out of Islam. There has been a vulgarization of Islam. Book-burning is not part of Islamic culture or teaching. I don't want to talk about Salman Rushdie. His book (*The Satanic Verses*) was terribly insulting, but I don't think any book should be banned. By banning a book we give it more publicity.

Muslims need to do a lot of introspection. And it is happening now. Young Muslims are coming forward and trying to spread awareness. We are fighting the old fundamentalist tendencies and leadership…and that's why I am talking to you today. But we need a platform. Our voices should be heard. Unfortunately, the media has played a very negative role. I've stopped reading newspapers altogether. But where there's a will there's a way, and we are determined to change the Muslim community for the better. *(As told to Hasan Suroor)*

ZULFKAR AHMAD (32), media and development consultant

Every individual has his own fears and struggles, and so has every community. When we look at our friends living in the neighbouring Muslim countries and the kind of fears and struggles they have, we feel quite blessed to be living in India. Like any other Indian citizen we enjoy every right guaranteed by the constitution of India, and are free to do what we want to without infringing anyone else's rights. However, that's how the larger picture looks, but when we look at the life of Muslims in India in detail, we get to notice a lot of qualms, fears, struggles, etc. both at the conscious and subconscious levels of mind. These fears keep permeating from conscious to subconscious, depending on the prevailing socio-economic conditions of Muslims and the reaction of the extremist chunk of the majority community to these conditions.

Being an Indian Muslim and a development professional, I don't need to refer to the findings of the Ranganath Mishra commission, Gopal Singh Committee, or Sachar Committee to know my socio-economic and political conditions because I know the prejudices associated with my name and how it feels to be a Kashmiri in the present scenario. I know how hard it is for a Muslim to find accommodation in any city, and if he is a Kashmiri, it becomes even more difficult. These prejudices do not just spring from nothing, they have been descending from generations to generations since long. They also vary from rural to urban, educated to uneducated, business class to bureaucracy and politics.

It is imperative here to understand the historical perspective of this problem. All these prejudices and mistrust have their roots in nearly 400 years of Muslim rule over India. Some of the incidents in those four hundred years hurt the religious sentiments of the Hindus, and that sentiment has passed from one century to the other. The most recent incident in history which strengthened the divide even further was the brutal massacre of men, women, children, old and young at the time of the partition of India. This unfortunate incident left some painfully indelible memories in the minds of people on both sides of the border. There are a few generations who have grown listening to these painful incidents of partition in India, and Pakistan as well. Consequently, we have a society filled with anger against the Muslims in India and Hindus in Pakistan. They look at Muslims with distrust and Muslims look at the majority community with suspicion. Ordinarily, this anger, mistrust, suspicion, etc. operate very subtly in India, but when it surfaces it takes the form of riots, which reignite and refresh the memories of the past and deepens the gap between the two communities. Immediately after such riots, life comes back to normal and the emotions of anger move from the conscious to the subconscious.

Normally, Muslims have to go an extra mile to prove their patriotism for India and now, after 9/11, there is a total change in the way people look at Muslims, not just in India but in every part of the world. Muslims have now mentally prepared themselves to get humiliated at airports, embassies, security checkpoints, etc. Sometimes our non-Muslim friends feel bad when they are let go at the airport and we are frisked twice and have to prove our identity beyond reasonable doubt. Being a Kashmiri Muslim, life is even more difficult as I have to face such humiliation almost every day. I could never imagine that my batch mates, friends, teachers at the university would oppose my election to the post of a General Secretary just on the basis of my religion and Kashmiri connection. Sometimes when I tell people how the Army burnt our house in Kashmir without any reason, they just don't accept it. Even my friends find it difficult to digest, but what gives me a sense of fairness and a tolerant democracy is that in India there is a small chunk of non-Muslims who understand the problems of Muslims and have come forward in support of the Muslims, not only on the ground but also to express their concern in print and electronic media.

When we analyse the overall situation, we see that Muslims are caught in a very tricky situation where their socio-economic and political growth is quite difficult, because the majority community does not find them trustworthy and the banks do not find them creditworthy. The prejudiced government policies towards Muslims have added to the trust deficit. To some extent, Muslims are also responsible for their backwardness as there is a severe leadership crisis in the community, and even after 65 years of independence, Muslims do not have a leader they can look up to. They are educationally backward hence their chances of economic or political growth are low. No leader has been able to help Muslims in India to keep pace with time. It's a proven fact that wherever Muslims in India have shown signs of growth, it was followed by communal riots like in Mumbai, Gujarat, etc. to not allow them to grow; and if you look at their representation in government jobs, it is abysmally low.

In spite of all the odds, Muslims hope that things will improve but it's not possible without a strong leadership. Young Muslims in India are conscious of the fact that change cannot be injected from outside, it has to come from within. We see a change in their approach as there are a number of organisations who are actively engaged in sensitising the Muslims in India and motivating them to join the civil services, politics, MNCs, etc. Muslims in India definitely need a leader who could do what Mian Fazli Hussain, the Education Minister in Dyarchy System did. He managed to get some quota reserved for Muslims in educational institutions which benefited the community greatly.

Later when he became the member of the executive council of the viceroy, he again managed to get some quota for Muslims in the Imperial service (Indian Civil Services). Most of the civil servants who had joined imperial services through the quota left for Pakistan in 1947, and Indian Muslims could never get such a benefit again; and as far the business class is concerned, their balance sheet could never become enviable.

In short, the government and the majority community have to understand that inclusive growth is not possible without integrating every section of the society. Minorities, particularly Muslims, need to understand the fact that the only way out is education, and they must use tools like Right to Information, Right to Education, Right to Equality, etc. and make concerted efforts to link themselves directly to the market as the best quality crafts, hand woven shawls, embroidery, needle work, etc. are produced by Muslims, and this could change their economic conditions to a great extent—hence empower them to take on the challenges of this century.

MARIA KHAN (24), student of Islamic studies

On the twentieth anniversary of the demotion of Babri Mosque I came across a link to an article by a prominent Indian Islamic scholar on Facebook. The article made an appeal to Muslims and human rights groups to recall the occasion as the greatest tragedy in the history of independent India. A young Muslim, commenting on the article, said the incident had happened decades ago, reigniting the negativities was of no avail and it was important to remain positive about what we already have and can achieve.

This observation by a Muslim reminded me of an article I

read, 'The Muslim as BJP supporter in Gujarat' (*The Hindu*, 24 February 2011). The author says: 'Religious symbolism became a shield for these Muslims to protect their identities against the threat of rising, rabid Hindutva. Compromise seemed impossible even in the exchange of economic development.' However, Muslims are now openly supporting and voting for the BJP in Gujarat. In the same article a Muslim is quoted as saying: 'If we do not assimilate with other communities, it's the end of us.'

The emotionally charged rhetoric and sloganeering done at Muslim gatherings, where the responsibility of one's problems is laid at the door of the other, no longer appeal to the educated young Muslims. Today the greatest concern of a person, Muslim or non-Muslim, is to build a good future for themselves and their family. And activities such as protests, demonstrations, and the politics of entitlement have yielded no results and, in fact, have proved to be counterproductive. Blaming others for one's plight and sitting with grievances doesn't help.

When the world is making vast strides in scientific advancement and economic progress, no young person would want to abandon being a part of these positive developments, and instead take to sloganeering. Even if a particular way of thinking prompts someone to do so, sooner or later they will realise their folly. Kashmir serves as a pertinent example, where, after the militancy which began around 1989, the economy deteriorated, businesses suffered tremendous losses, education of the future generations was compromised, and the flourishing tourism industry that provided sustenance for the Kashmiri people was jeopardized. A Kashmiri trader once said that there were no buyers for Kashmiri apples.

The Kashmiri people are now beginning to realize that they

had come under the influence of misguided political leaders and by answering their call they were led on the road to their own ruination. Militancy has considerably decreased in Kashmir today, life is returning back to normal, and tourism is again gaining strength, with around one million tourists visiting Kashmir in the year 2011.

This is the trend we see among Muslims in India today. By dint of sheer hard work and struggle, Muslims are making their mark in various fields. When this change of mindset occurs, the same country, which till yesterday was a land of problems, transforms into a land of opportunities. Through the availing of these opportunities any person can carve a bright future for himself. It is internal consolidation that has given Muslims anything substantial, and not externally targeted protestations.

In June 2011, I happened to meet a Pakistani woman who now lives in the U.S. We were discussing the condition of Muslims in India. She remarked, in a casual tone, that in India discrimination against Muslims was commonplace. I told her that I was also a Muslim and I too had been living in the same India all my life, and not once did I face discrimination for being a Muslim. In India Muslims have all the scope to develop in any field. If Muslims are not developing, it is because they are themselves failing to positively utilize what India has to offer them. And, as the Quran says: 'Whatever misfortune befalls you is of your own doing.'(42:30)

Another issue that figures very prominently in Muslim newspapers is what is termed as profiling, or random arrests of innocent Muslim youths in terror-related cases. On going through these reports, which one will inevitably find in Muslim magazines and journals, one feels that Muslims are extremely innocent people who are unilaterally being made subject of others' conspiracies.

It is very important to analyze and understand this situation. This is what is usually called stereotyping Muslims, and is discussed at length on popular news channels. We hear that innocent Muslim boys are arrested after terrorist incidents. Immense hue and cry is made in the aftermath of these incidents, but are Muslims really as innocent as they are portrayed in Muslim newspapers, and the other party outright conspirators? No. There is no denying the fact that Muslims are engaged in perpetrating terrorism, the most notorious in the recent past being the 26/11 Mumbai attacks in which over 100 people were killed. The accused in the attacks were all Muslims, even if they were Pakistanis.

If members of a community are engaged in such violent activities in the name of their religion, they become a reason for other members of their community to be cast in the same light. Thus it is the responsibility of Muslims, particularly Islamic scholars, to condemn these terrorist activities done in the name of Islam. The extremist ideology promises heaven to those Muslims who engage in violence, which is wrongly termed jihad. It is this ideology that motivates Muslims to do violence. An ideology can be countered only by an ideology. Here the ulema or scholars have to play their part. A peaceful counter-ideology has to be provided to make this violent ideology ineffective and unappealing to the Muslims. Islam should be presented to all as a religion of peace. Muslims must unilaterally throw away all their arms and strictly follow the path of non-confrontation. In doing so, they will take away the justification from others for holding them responsible for any violence.

Another important responsibility of Muslim leaders is to give up the mentality of hatred and negativity for the other community. People from other communities are as human as we are. The Quran refers to God as the 'God of all mankind' not as the 'God of Muslims'. The concept of 'we and they' is totally un-Islamic.

If Muslims want to play a constructive role in India they have to shun all negativities, stop imagining conspiracy theories, and live with their fellow countrymen in a spirit of brotherhood and harmony.

FAZAL AHMED (26), self-employed salesman

There's no point pretending that being a Muslim in India is easy. I grew up under the shadow of the demolition of Babri Masjid and the post-9/11 anti-Muslim campaign, which is still reflected in the way Muslims are treated by the police and other security forces. Hundreds of innocent Muslims have been thrown behind bars on mostly trumped up charges of terrorism. Panic spreads in the Muslim community whenever there is a terrorist incident because they know what will happen next: more young Muslims will be picked up and sent to prison. Then, of course, there is the well-known problem of discrimination in jobs and housing. I have been refused houses because I'm a Muslim. They don't say that, of course. They say they want only vegetarians or some such thing. Having said that, I am not in favour of constantly moaning and groaning about it. We have been doing that for years, but where has it got us? Political parties have made use of us for votes by exploiting emotional issues. No political party is genuinely interested in Muslim welfare. So, simply by complaining we are not going to get anywhere. I am not saying that we should not fight for our rights, but there are lots of things we can do ourselves. Nobody is stopping us from sending our children to school. Nobody is telling us: don't educate your daughters. Nobody is preventing us from being more tolerant. The reason we are not taken seriously is because we are so weak and have nothing to show for ourselves.

We must first set our own house in order and see what we can do to help ourselves. And there's a lot we can do. Instead of waiting for jobs to fall in our laps on the basis of second- and third-class university degrees, we must study market trends, look for skills that employers need, and then develop them. There is a growing building industry which requires a whole range of skills. Then of course there's the IT industry, and I am not talking about high-end technology but at the basic level. There's manufacturing. There is a big catering and hospitality sector. We have been too busy chasing white collar jobs with our BA (pass) degrees. What we need instead is vocational training that will equip us for many of the jobs that we never think of. The future is 'blue', not 'white'.

Once we have skills we can set up our own small businesses. I know it is not easy to get bank loans but there are plenty of rich Muslims and they should come forward and fund good business ideas. They have a social responsibility. The whole community will have to pull together if it wants to get itself out of the hole. We should learn from other communities. Look at Sikhs; look at Parsis.

We should stop complaining about discrimination. The job market is so competitive that employers are spoilt for choice. Why should they settle for the second or third best if they can get the best? Muslims will have to make sure they are the best if they want jobs. Mind you, it is not only Muslims who are not getting jobs. Every time a Muslim is refused job, there are also several non-Muslims who have been rejected. If it is the case that Muslims don't get jobs only because of their religion then why are millions of non-Muslims unemployed?

There may be problems, but India is my country. There is no other place I can call my own. I have never been abroad but I know I will be terribly homesick anywhere else. I am not saying that I will never consider going abroad for a better future but it will have no bearing on my love for my country. I don't have to prove my patriotism to anyone. If there are people who think they alone have a monopoly over patriotism simply because they are in a majority, my answer is: dream on…
(*Translated from Urdu*)

CASSANDRA (28), media student

If war can be a 'lovely' thing why can't be it fun to be a Muslim? What did you say Sir? I must be joking? No, I am not. I have done it and it works. And since you asked, let me confess that I too was like you once. Always moaning about Islamophobia and the plight of Muslims. I had convinced myself that because I was a Muslim the whole world was against me, and there were Muslim-haters lurking in every corner. I was always angry and would become defensive at any criticism of Muslims. Now that I look back, I find myself laughing at my own stupidity. It was all in my mind. I became even more paranoid when I read reports about passengers with Muslim-sounding names being offloaded from planes because other passengers, suspecting them to be terrorists, wouldn't fly with them. I became so conscious of my name that I hesitated to disclose it, and then when I did I waited to see the reaction. Often I imagined the other person smirk as though saying: 'Oh, here we go again... another Muslim to deal with...' My paranoia deepened after an incident which, in retrospect, seems laughable. But at the time I saw it as another proof of Islamophobia. One day I got a call from a consumer survey firm. There was a girl on the line and she asked if I would answer some questions. It would just take a 'few minutes', she assured me. After I had answered most of the questions she came to the last query: to which of the following religious groups do you belong? With some trepidation I said: Muslim. Immediately the girl said: sorry, in that case we need you to answer a few more questions...it will just take another few minutes. Upon which I lost my temper and hung up...For days afterwards I found myself retelling the story to anyone who cared to listen. While non-Muslims laughed saying more questions must have been meant to get a 'better understanding' of Muslim consumers' shopping habits, Muslims, without exception, agreed that there was something 'sinister' about it. One said they must be collecting more information about Muslims because they suspect 'we are all terrorists'.

So, sir, believe me, I was like you once. Obsessed with conspiracy theories and constantly worried about the 'fate' of Muslims. But all that is behind me. Now I am having fun being a Muslim. What sir? How did I change? Oh, you won't believe it if I tell you that it just happened overnight. Literally. One day I was watching TV and there was this man from some Muslim organisation going on and on about how Muslims were being 'terrorised' in the name of fighting terrorism. Suddenly something snapped within me. Why, on a lovely day like this, when everyone else looked happy and bright, was this man bent on making us Muslims feel so miserable? For a moment I wondered if he and other self-pitying Muslims were in cahoots with Muslim-bashers to make us unhappy. Were they part of a larger conspiracy to torment us? It was a eureka moment for me. I switched off the television and decided that enough was enough. No more wallowing in self-pity. No more moaning about Islamophobia. And no more angst about being a Muslim. To hell with Muslim-haters and to hell with Muslim cry babies. I am not going to let them spoil my party. I am going to have fun being a Muslim. And since then I have done just that. Trust me, sir, it is that simple once you decide to take the plunge.

So, let's get on with it. For starters, say damn to Islamophobia. Don't give a second thought to that gleaming, long beard of yours which precedes you at airport immigration. No need to tinker with that give-away name of yours which starts with Mohammed or ends with Ahmed. And those hijabs are just fine. What the hell if others think that you look like a walking-talking separatist. Islamic identity is important to you and you'll of course flaunt it! Enjoy being a Muslim while Islamophobia lasts!

(Cassandra is a pseudonym)

Postscript

A big collateral casualty of religious fundamentalism has been the Muslim sense of humour. Muslims were not always so humourless. Mughal emperors were great patrons of humour. One of emperor Akbar's favourite courtiers was Birbal, a man with a legendary sense of ready wit. Some of India's most famous Muslim poets were known not only for their humour but irreverence towards religion and, indeed, God.

Religion appears to have had the same paralyzing effect on Muslim humour as love had on Mirza Ghalib who famously wrote: *Ishq ne Ghalib nikamma kar diya, warna hum bhi aadmi the kaam ke* (love has made me absolutely useless, otherwise I was also once capable of great things). When barred by mullahs from drinking in the vicinity of a mosque, he told them: '*zahid sharab peene de masjid mein baith ke, ya woh jaggah pade de jahan khuda no ho*' (o priest, let me sit and drink inside the mosque or tell me that place where God can't be found).

On another occasion, mocking the idea of angels deciding man's fate, he sighed and said: '*Pakde jaate hain farishton ke likhe par naahaq aadmi koi hamara dam-e-tahrir bhi thaa*' (we are punished simply on the say-so of angels, shouldn't there be a fellow human being to decide our fate).

Zauq wrote: '*Zauq! Jo medresse ke bigre hue hain mulla, Un ko maikhaane mein le aao sanwar jaayenge*' (Zauq! bring the mulla misled by a madrassa to the tavern, it will correct his ways).

In today's climate, these poets might have been lynched

for taking such liberties with things spiritual.

The good news, however, is that a smile is returning to the Indian Muslim's face. Shazia Mirza, the British stand-up comic who has often upset her co-religionists at home, got 'ecstatic' response from Indian Muslims. Young Muslims joke how Islamophobia has made Muslims 'famous' overnight.

'Badnaam bhi honge to kya naam na hoga' (even notoriety means a sort of fame), was how a poetic-minded Muslim broadcaster put it.

My young nephew, who has a beard, cheerily dismisses his frequent run-ins with immigration officials at Heathrow airport as 'VIP treatment'. One journalism student asked me if I could help him publish a humorous piece he had written called 'Oh! To be a Muslim', arguing that if a war could be 'lovely' (a reference to the musical film *Oh!What a Lovely War*) why couldn't it be 'fun' being a Muslim in an age of Islamophobia. When, instead, I offered to include it in my book he said: 'But I don't want my name please. My family may not like it.' So it appears under the pseudonym, Cassandra (see *In their Own Words*).

But religion remains a 'no-go' area even for the most liberal Muslims. They draw a line at 'fooling around' with Islam or its important figures. That's the Rubicon they are not yet ready to cross.

The important point though is that things are changing, and, as a poet said, *'Un ko baton mein laga laaye to hain, aur khul jayenge do chaar mulaqaton mein'* (we have brought them along this far, hopefully we'll get there soon...).

Appendix 1

What It Means to be a Muslim in India Today: A Combined Report of People's Tribunal on the Atrocities Committed Against the Minorities in The Name of Fighting Terrorism (22-24 August 2008 at Hyderabad) & National Meet on the Status of Muslims in Contemporary India (Delhi 3 to 5 Oct 2009) *Edited by* Shabnam Hashmi for *Act Now for Harmony and Democracy* (ANHAD)

Last decade (2000-2010) saw multiple acts of terror in different parts of India. These attacks were scattered in different parts of India and killed many innocent people. The attack on Parliament, blast near the Army camp in Jammu, terror episode at Akshardham, Mumbai trains and Sankatmochan temple are a few among the many terror acts which took place. Along with the loss of many innocent lives, the social atmosphere was vitiated. These blasts intimidated the society as a whole and created an atmosphere of fear all around. During this period, on the heels of the World Trade Center attack, the word Islamic terrorism was coined and in India this word was further manipulated to highly dubious and wrong propaganda line that 'All Terrorists are Muslims.'

India had witnessed massive anti-Muslim violence from the decade of 1980s, culminating in the post-demolition anti-Muslim violence and the Gujarat violence of 2002. The loss of property and lives of Muslim community was abysmal. The lives lost of the community were more than 80 per cent of the total victims, the victims were not rehabilitated by the state, no adequate compensation and no justice was meted out to most of the victims.

The Muslim community started feeling dejected to a great extent with the violence and the consequent harassment, leading to the sense of insecurity.

In this background, in most cases, after the blasts many a Muslim youth were arrested on the charges of being involved in the act of terror; of being in league with the Pakistan terror groups. The investigation authorities recklessly arrested Muslim youth after every act of terror. Young Muslim boys and men were subjected to torture, encountered and remained in police custody for months.

Meanwhile, from April 2006, the deaths of two Bajrang Dal men while they were making bombs came to light in Nanded, Maharashtra. This was followed by a series of terror attacks in Parbhani, Aurangabad, Jalna, Panvel etc.—in these cases the involvement of Hindutva groups was apparent to a great deal. Still the investigating agencies kept working with the same assumption that Muslims were behind all terror attacks. The twin fact of being victims of communal violence and later victims of police investigation, a sense of despair started gripping the Muslim community. There was hardly any evidence needed, and police investigations were based on the flight of their imagination around the understanding that if there is an act of terror, the Muslims have to be involved. The despair amongst the Muslim community became much worse after the realization that while Muslim congregations were attacked or bombs planted in Muslim majority areas, still the Muslims were suspected for these acts and put behind bars and tortured to elicit confession. Muslim youth studying in professional colleges and other disciplines were also not spared. The sense of hopelessness was too strong and it started getting worse for the psyche of the Muslim community as a whole.

Meanwhile their economic plight was made public by the

Sachar Committee report, published in 2006. The report, based on concrete data, made it clear that during the last six decades after independence the conditions of Muslims as a community has deteriorated. Their economic status, social conditions, political say and representation, all faced a severe jolt, and the community started feeling as if they are being pushed into being second class citizens. Many a delegations met the political leaders concerned. The appeal to put the investigation on an honest ground fell on deaf ears and the police continued to arrest and torture. The case of Samjhauta Express blast, Ajmer Dargah and Mecca Masjid in Hyderabad were most glaring in this regard. So the community faced twin challenges, on one hand being branded as terrorists and on the other, communal elements intensified their propaganda against the Muslim community. This further intensified the process of marginalization of the Muslim community. The twin aspects of security and equity got a severe setback and the community was in total despair. Even the most liberal and educated sections of Muslims started feeling that they could not live in peace and with dignity in this atmosphere.

During the same period the infiltration of the communal mindset in the system and its influence on a large section of media, started becoming more obvious. A small section of national media did expose this nexus but a larger section of the media kept carrying the police versions of the events and the communal demonization of Muslim community. Some independent social activists and groups did raise their voice against what was going on, but their impact was not very palpable.

It is in this frightening backdrop that we at Anhad decided to make an attempt to shake the national conscience, to share the pain and anguish of the Muslim community with a larger section of the society, to project the voice of the voiceless to the authorities and political leadership. In this direction both these tribunals were organized. The first one, 'Peoples Tribunal on the Atrocities Committed against Minorities In the name of Fighting Terrorism', was held from 22-24 August 2008 at Hyderabad. This focused mainly on the victims of police investigations around acts of terrorism. And the second one, 'National Meet on the Status of Muslims in Contemporary India', held in Delhi from 3-5 October 2009 focused on the overall situation of the community in the national scenario.

The findings of the tribunals were quite revealing about the condition of the Muslim minorities. Many a testimonies moistened the eyes of the jury members—the harrowing stories of mothers whose sons are being tortured; wives whose husbands were made victims of police atrocities; the third degree torture in police custody; the insensitivity of the administration—was all there, and was registered with the pain and objectivity it deserved. The jury was unanimous in giving the interim report and conclusions. It is difficult to assess the impact of the tribunal as such, but in the aftermath of the tribunal it seemed that the reckless arrests of Muslim youth stopped to some extent; while the government is yet to gives hope to the comprehensive policies which should give Muslim their rightful due in the society. We are publishing the proceedings of the tribunal in a single volume, as though the themes of the tribunal may sound different, they are deeply connected and supplementary. These reports are a mirror of the society, a mirror to our democracy. These reports should remind us that no democracy is worth its principles unless the minorities can live with security and dignity in that community. Time alone will tell the direction of the social policies but we do realize that we have to keep up the battle for democratic rights for the minorities, as the state on its own has not been performing its constitutional duty of being fair and just to the minorities. The tasks for human rights workers are immense as we have a long way to go to be able to democratize the society, to ensure that the values of our freedom movement, the values of the Constitution, are upheld and practiced at all the levels.

—From foreword by Ram Punyani

Appendix 2

Findings and Recommendations

The testimonies showed that a large number of innocent young Muslims have been and are being victimized by the police on charges of being involved in various terrorist acts across the country.

This is particularly so in Maharashtra, Gujarat, Madhya Pradesh, Andhra Pradesh and Rajasthan, though not limited to these states.

In most of the cases, the persons picked up are not shown to be arrested by the police until many days after their arrest, in gross violation of the law. Their families are also not informed about their arrest. In many cases, they have been tortured in police custody and made to 'confess' and sign blank papers. The police has often been humiliating to Muslim détentes on the ground of their religion.

The testimonies show widespread communalization of the police across states in the country.

In most of these cases the courts are routinely allowing police remand and not granting bail, merely on police statements that the accused are required for further investigation. They do not examine whether there is any evidence against the accused. Unfortunately, the media too uncritically publicizes the charges and allegations levelled by the police. This has resulted in the destruction of lives and reputations of a large number of people so picked up by the police, who have later been found to be innocent.

When the police chargesheets the victims, the trials go on almost interminably during which the poor victims are virtually defenceless since they are often not even able to get lawyers. In some cases, Bar Associations have been preventing lawyers from appearing on behalf of persons accused by the police of such terror offences. However, though this is a gross contempt of the court, the courts have not taken action against such Bar Associations and lawyers who are coercing other lawyers in this manner.

Even when the victims are acquitted or discharged on being found innocent, they are not compensated for the destruction of their lives and reputations. Even when the case against the victim is found to be totally cooked up, no action is being taken to hold the concerned police officials accountable. This has led to impunity among the police officials as a result of which they are casually and callously picking up and victimizing innocent persons, particularly Muslims, sometimes even to extract money from them.

It has been reported by the victims that those citizens who are picked up by police officers for interrogation and are subjected to repeated harassment and torture, are implicated in false cases even after release or acquittal, and are further subjected to mental and physical torture.

Unfortunately, the courts are going along with this behaviour of the police and are virtually ignoring allegations of torture in police custody. Hardly anyone is being held accountable for the torture and third degree methods that are being routinely practiced by the police, and even in judicial custody.

Unfortunately the Human Rights Commissions, which should have taken suo motto cognizance of such victimization and violation of human rights of these people, have by and large been treating complaints with casual indifference. They either do not take up such cases on the ground that they are the subject matter of court proceedings, or just ask for a routine police report without getting any independent investigation done on such serious charges of human rights violations. This victimization and demonisation of Muslims in the guise of investigation of terror offences, is having a very serious psychological impact on the minds of not only the families of the victims but also other members of the community. It is leading to a very strong sense of insecurity and alienation, which may lead to frightful consequences for the nation.

Appendix 3

Sachar Committee Report

Social, Economic and Educational Status of the Muslim Community in India

Main Recommendations

- Mechanisms to ensure equity and equality of opportunity and eliminate discrimination.
- Creation of a National Data Bank (NDB) where all relevant data for various Socio Religious Communities are maintained.
- Form an autonomous Assessment and Monitoring Authority to evaluate the extent of development benefits.
- An Equal Opportunity Commission should be constituted to look into the grievances of the deprived groups.
- Elimination of the anomalies with respect to reserved constituencies under the delimitation scheme.
- The idea of providing certain incentives to a diversity index should be explored to ensure equal opportunities in education, governance, private employment and housing.
- A process of evaluating the content of school textbooks needs to be initiated and institutionalized.
- The UGC should evolve a system where part of the allocation to colleges and universities is linked to the diversity in the student population.

- Providing hostel facilities at reasonable costs for students from minorities must be taken up on a priority basis.
- The Committee recommended promoting and enhancing access to Muslims in Priority Sector Bank Advances.
- The real need is of policy initiatives that improve the participation and share of the Minorities, particularly Muslims, in the business of regular commercial banks.
- The community should be represented on interview panels and Boards. The underprivileged should be helped to utilize new opportunities in its high growth phase through skill development and education.
- Provide financial and other support to initiatives built around occupations where Muslims are concentrated, and have growth potential.

Appendix 4

Excerpts from Chapter 12

Looking Ahead: Perspectives and Recommendations

1. The Context

This report has probed the question of whether different socio-religious categories (SRCs) in India have had an equal chance to reap the benefits of development, with a focus on Muslims in India. It was stated at the outset that minorities have to grapple with issues relating to identity, security and equity. It was also recognized that these three sets of issues are inter-related. Since the mandate of this Committee is primarily on equality, the Report essentially deals with the relative deprivation of Muslims vis-a-vis other SRCs in various dimensions of development. It may also be useful to recall the distinction made in the introductory chapter between issues that are common to all poor people and those that are specific to minorities, especially Muslims.

Our analysis shows that while there is considerable variation in the conditions of Muslims across states, (and among Muslims, those who identified themselves as OBCs and others), the Community exhibits deficits and deprivation in practically all dimensions of development. In fact, by and large, Muslims are somewhat above SCs/STs but below Hindu-OBCs, other minorities, and Hindu-general (mostly upper castes) in almost all indicators considered. Among the states that have large Muslim populations the situation is particularly grave in the states of West Bengal, Bihar, Uttar Pradesh and Assam. Interestingly, despite such deficits, the Community has lower infant mortality rates and sex-ratios. In addition to the 'development deficit', the perception among Muslims that they are discriminated against and excluded is widespread, which exacerbates the problem.

The Committee strongly suggests that the policies to deal with the relative deprivation of the Muslims in the country should sharply focus on inclusive development and 'mainstreaming' of the Community, while respecting diversity. There is an urgent need to recognise diversity in residential, work, and educational spaces, apart from enhancing inclusion of the really deprived SRCs in 'spaces' created by public programmes and policy interventions. The need for equality and inclusion in a pluralistic society can never be over-emphasised. But the mechanisms to ensure equality of opportunity to bring about inclusion should be such that diversity is achieved, and at the same time the perception of discrimination is eliminated. This is only possible when the importance of Muslims as an intrinsic part of the diverse Indian social mosaic is squarely recognized.

Given this context, the policy perspectives and recommendations discussed below fall into two broad categories:

- General policy Initiatives/approaches that cut across different aspects of socio-economic and educational development analysed in the Report; and
- Specific policy measures that deal with particular issues and/or dimensions (e.g. education, credit, etc.), covered in the Report.

2. General Policy Initiatives and Approaches:

We discuss here a set of over-arching initiatives that are of importance on their own and would also enhance the efficacy of more specific instruments discussed later;

2.1 Need for Transparency, Monitoring and Data Availability:

Availability of reliable data on a continuing basis across SRCs on socio-economic conditions, government programmes, and the like is critical fordesigning appropriate policies, ensuring transparency, and effectively monitoringvarious initiatives and programmes. In other words: availability of detailed data is a prerequisite for good governance. Availability of such data would also make policy instruments like Right to Information Act more efficacious. The Committee had faced the acute problem of non-availability of reliable data and, therefore, had to launch an independent effort to collect, collate, and consolidate available data.

The data obtained through these mechanisms with considerable difficulty was still not exhaustive enough to analyse several issues to our satisfaction. There is an immediate need, therefore, to make arrangements to collect data for different SRCs on a regular basis and make it available to researchers and the public.

We recommend a creation of a National Data Bank (NOB) where all relevant data for various SRCs are maintained. All the data should be eventually computerized and made available on the Internet. The Census, the National Accounts Statistics (NAS), and NSSO are the most important sources of large scale good quality data but they are not able to readily provide data on crucial variables to assess the social, economic, and educational conditions according to SRCs. There is an urgent need, therefore, to assess afresh the data needs for evaluating conditions of citizens by SRC status on a regular basis so as to understand and assess the flow of development benefits. The NDB should also be the repository of data on different beneficiary-oriented government programmes undertaken at the national and state levels along with the details of beneficiaries drawn from different SRCs. Details of employment, credit flows, programme participation, etc. should also be shared by various national and state agencies and undertakings with the NDB.

For this purpose, the NDB should have the resources and authority to access data from other agencies identified above as well as to obtain required information from government departments, both at the Centre and at the state levels. In fact, it should be obligatory on the part of the relevant departments of the central and state governments to supply the information to the NDB. While the Central Statistical Commission, which has been set up recently, could provide the broad framework, the NDB should function as an autonomous body.

Once such data are available there is a need to institutionalize the mechanisms for assessment and monitoring in order to suggest policy options on a timely basis.

The Committee recommends the setting up of an autonomous Assessment and Monitoring Authority (AMA) to evaluate the extent of development benefits which accrue to different SRCs through various programmes. Academics, professionals, civil society organizations along with state authorities as the official members, can be part of this Authority and perform a watch-dog function, which closely monitors the participation of various SRCs in both state and central level programme implementation. As the government and public records are being digitized it would be possible for the AMA to monitor 'diversity', in participation, on a regular basis. The digitizatlon will also facilitate monitoring at all levels of governance, particularly the panchayats and nagarpalikas, districts, and of course the states and the Centre. While monitoring should be done on a concurrent basis, an elaborate monitoring exercise should be undertaken every five years. The results of this exercise can be profitably utilized for reformulation of policies, if required.

2.2 Enhancing the Legal Basis for Providing Equal Opportunities:

The widespread perception of discrimination among the Muslim community needs to be addressed. There are hardly any empirical studies that establish discrimination. Research in this area needs to be encouraged, but is particularly difficult at the moment due to non-availability of data. Hopefully, better availability of data would result in more studies in this area. While equality in the implementation of programmes and better participation of the Community in the development process would gradually eliminate this perception of discrimination, there is a need to strengthen the legal provisions to eliminate such cases.

The Indian Constitution in 'Part-III - Fundamental Rights' has exhaustively provided not only for equality of all citizens irrespective of their religion but has also provided special provisions for protecting the rights of minorities in respect of their religion, language, and culture. Thus, any violation of the rights of the minority by the states could be challenged in a court of law. There are also institutions like the National Human Rights Commission (NHRC) and National Commission for Minorities (NCM) to look into complaints made by the minorities with respect to the State action. But these mechanisms can *only* have a limited role and cannot look into many complaints arising on a day-to-day basis against non-state agencies. The minorities, many a time, may feel that there is discrimination against them in the matter of employment, housing, for obtaining loans from the public or private sector banks, or opportunities for good schooling.

It is self-evident that if minorities have these perceptions, law must provide an effective mechanism which should examine their complaints, and be able to give effective relief. It is imperative that if the minorities have certain perceptions of being aggrieved, all efforts should be made by the State to find a mechanism by which these complaints could be attended to expeditiously. This mechanism should operate in a manner which gives full satisfaction to the minorities that any denial of equal opportunities or bias or discrimination in dealing with them by a public functionary or any private individual, will immediately be attended to and redressal given. Such a mechanism should be accessible to all individuals and institutions desirous to complain that they have received less favourable treatment from any employer or any person on the basis of his/her SRC background and gender. It is wrong to assume that there is an inevitable conflict between the interests of the majority and minority communities in the country. This is flawed reasoning and assumption. Deprivation, poverty, and discrimination may exist among all SRCs although in different proportions. But the fact of belonging to a minority community has, it cannot be denied, an in-built sensitivity to discrimination. This sensitivity is natural and may exist among religious minorities in any country. Recognizing this reality is not pandering to the minorities, nor sniping at the majority. This recognition is only an acceptance of reality. 'It is a well-accepted maxim in law that not only must justice be done, but it must appear to be done.' It is in that context the Committee recommends that an Equal Opportunity Commission (EOC) should be constituted by the government to look into the grievances of the deprived groups. An example of such a policy tool is the UK Race Relations Act, 1976. While providing a redressal mechanism for different types of discrimination, this will give a further re-assurance to the minorities that any unfair action against them will invite the vigilance of the law.

Appendix 5

UPA Government's 15-point Programme for Minorities

1. Equitable availability of the Integrated Child Development Services (ICDS).
2. Improving access to school education.
3. Greater resources for teaching Urdu.
4. Modernizing Madrassa education.
5. Scholarships for meritorious students from minority communities.
6. Improving educational infrastructure through the Maulana Azad Education Foundation.
7. Self-employment and wage employment for the poor.
8. Upgradation of skill through technical training.
9. Enhanced credit support for economic activities.
10. Recruitment to state and central services.
11. Equitable share in rural housing scheme.
12. Improvement in condition of slums inhabited by minority communities.
13. Prevention of communal incidents.
14. Prosecution for communal offences.
15. Rehabilitation of victims of communal riots.

Acknowledgements

This book is an outcome of my long professional and personal engagement with the 'Muslim Question'. I owe a debt to all my friends, colleagues and family members who helped me clarify my understanding of the many issues surrounding the contentious debate around Indian Muslims.

In particular, I would like to thank Rashmee Roshan Lall for her forthright views during our long conversations, which invariably ended in an argument. Her reaction to my 'Muslim Spring' theory is likely to be a rather bemused, 'interesting'.

Special thanks are due to Suchitra Behal who read the first draft and encouraged me to 'go for it'.

I also wish to thank Neena Vyas and V. Krishna Ananth for helping me with their analysis of the turbulent communal politics of the 1980s and 1990s; and Seema Chishti for taking me through current electoral trends. There is a long list of people to whom I owe a debt of gratitude, not least to my interviewees who took time out to speak to me at length. Saif Mahmood and Mehar Rahman provided invaluable material for my research. Rahat Abrar and his colleagues at Aligarh Muslim University were very kind and helpful. Arshad Rahman and Asad encouraged me to gatecrash into Darul Uloom Nadwa, Lucknow.

I also wish to thank Shabnam Hashmi for allowing me to reproduce extracts from *What It Means to be a Muslim in India Today* brought out by Act Now for Harmony and Democracy (ANHAD).

I am grateful to my publishers Rupa Publications India, particularly its managing director, Mr R.K. Mehra who I first got to know some thirty years ago when, as a young reporter with *The Statesman* in Delhi, I ran an occasional book column and he spoilt me for choice with supplies of new titles.

Last, but not the least, it was a great learning experience working with my editor, Elina Majumdar, whose valuable suggestions helped shape a tentative manuscript into a coherent and 'proper' book.